To

Grannan

I hope you enjoy my book!

Lauren

P.S Merry christmas 2002

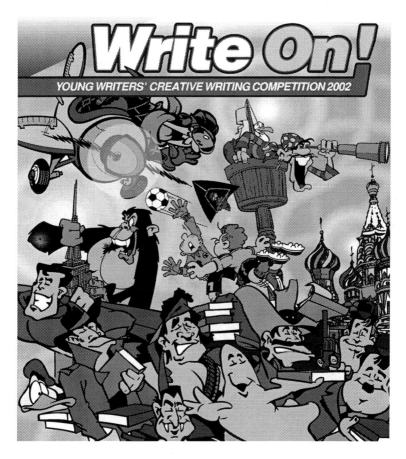

EASTERN COUNTIES VOL II

Edited by Claire Tupholme

First published in Great Britain in 2002 by
YOUNG WRITERS
Remus House,
Coltsfoot Drive,
Peterborough, PE2 9JX
Telephone (01733) 890066

HB ISBN 0 75434 022 8
SB ISBN 0 75434 023 6

FOREWORD

This year, Young Writers proudly presents a showcase of the best short stories and creative writing from today's up-and-coming writers.

We set the challenge of writing for one of our four themes - 'General Short Stories', 'Ghost Stories', 'Tales With A Twist' and 'A Day In The Life Of . . .'. The effort and imagination expressed by each individual writer was more than impressive and made selecting entries an enjoyable, yet demanding, task.

Write On! Eastern Counties Vol II is a collection that we feel you are sure to enjoy - featuring the very best young authors of the future. Their hard work and enthusiasm clearly shines within these pages, highlighting the achievement each story represents.

We hope you are as pleased with the final selection as we are and that you will continue to enjoy this special collection for many years to come.

CONTENTS

The Stories

HOUSE OF THE DEAD

It was a dark night. James heard noises in his closet. He rushed to his mum and dad's room and stayed there for the night.

There was a mansion across the road from where James lived. Nobody had ever been in it, as it was scary. There were noises outside the window at dinner time as the zombie was creeping around. When Dad was doing the washing up the zombie got a stabbing knife and nearly killed him.

The next day James and his friends went to explore the mansion. They heard noises and followed them into the attic. They saw a coffin. It slipped over and they climbed out of the window. They peeped in and saw a zombie and a mummy. They started chasing after James, Adam and John. They got safely back into their homes.

In the morning James went to school. He told the class but nobody believed him. He wanted to show them but he did not know how. That night he went to look at the mansion, there was nothing there, it was all too quiet. The zombies came out and surrounded him. He thought he was going to die but it was all a dream . . .

George Hopkin (9)
Avon House School, Woodford Green, Essex

DANIEL'S FIRST HUNT

Daniel is eight years old. He likes playing football. He and his dad planned to go hunting. Daniel was excited. It was his first hunt. They went next morning and before they went Daniel said goodbye to his mother.

They went in the morning and went to the woods for where they were going to hunt. A few hours later they were hunting. They each had guns. It was Daniel's first time to use a gun and he was nervous.
Dad said, 'Pull the trigger at the deer which is running by.'
Daniel pulled the trigger nervously and released the bullet strike end.
Daniel jumped up and down in amazement as he shot the deer.
His dad said, 'Well done Daniel, now you've got the hang of it.

After they were hungry so they cooked the deer and ate some of it. The next morning they brushed their teeth and ate the rest of the deer for breakfast. They then went on their journey to kill another creature. They walked for an hour and they couldn't find any animals on the ground.

In the night Dad shot a deer. They ate some of it. Next morning Daniel and Dad came home. Mum was happy to see them.

Varun Kirpal (8)
Avon House School, Woodford Green, Essex

THE HOLIDAY THAT GOT SPOILT

There was once two girls, their names were Sarah and Jenna. They were both cousins. Jenna was twenty-four and Sarah was twenty-one. They were celebrating their birthdays. The country they were going to was the South of France for a year. They were going to drive there and rent a house. They were going by themselves.

The day before they were going away, they packed. They were flatmates so it was easier to see what they needed to take and they were learning French from their book.

Soon they had packed. Sarah went to the kitchen, it was small because they lived in a flat. Ten minutes before Sarah had put sausages in to a frying pan. Sarah took the sausages out of the frying pan and put them on plates. Soon Jenna came in and made the drinks which were orange squash. After tea they went to bed after they had brushed their teeth.

In the night something amazing happened. Two people came from the street into Sarah and Jenna's house, the people in their house were called Spoilt Samantha and her fiancée Moaning Michael. Their worst nightmare. Suddenly there was a *thud, thud, thud, bang, bang*, that woke Sarah and Jenna up. Both said, 'Quickly you go and get the torch then check the money cupboard.' That's where Sarah and Jenna kept their precious bits and bobs, while Jenna checked the house to see who it was. It was Spoilt Samantha and Moaning Michael.
'Good afternoon,' Jenna said rudely. 'So it's Samantha and Michael.'

Suddenly Sarah came rushing in with the police and the Prime Minister (Sarah's dad) and Lou, Sarah and Jenna's puppy. And that was their worst holiday, because Michael and Samantha had put the tickets somewhere and they were never found and they didn't go away.

Rebecca Cox (8)
Avon House School, Woodford Green, Essex

SABRINA'S ADVENTURE 2002

Sabrina is a baby puppy. She loves adventures. She lives in Animal World.

'Come on Sabrina darling!' exclaimed Sabrina's mum (whose name is Gem).'If you don't hurry then you will arrive at the party very late!'
'OK, OK!' cried Sabrina. She came walking down the stairs calmly.

Gem and Sabrina walked together to the party. Soon she heard a peculiar noise. She thought that maybe it could be one of her cheeky friends trying to scare her or even trying to play hide-and-seek. But to her dismay it was a snake! 'Uh oh,' Sabrina said. She had to walk through the jungle to reach the party.
The snake said, 'You would do fine for my tummy.'
'Uh oh, thank you, um I think I have to help my mum with quite a bit of shopping.'

Sabrina ran as fast as her legs could take her. 'Oh no, where is my mum!' whined Sabrina. 'Oh no, where is my mum . . .'
'Squawk!'
'Who said that?' Sabrina asked curiously.
'Me, Polly!'
'Have you seen my mummy?' exclaimed Sabrina.
'I saw her looking very worried.'
'Thank you!' Sabrina said overjoyed.
She soon saw her mum.
'Hi Mum!'

Radhika Bhanot (8)
Avon House School, Woodford Green, Essex

BABY DOLPHIN IN DANGER

One snowy morning I went to the beach. I wanted to go snorkelling so my dad went to get the things for me. When I got my clothes on I dived into the water, it was very cold. As I got closer I saw some upset dolphins. I was wondering why they were so upset. Then I saw why. I swam closer. I swam quickly to the baby dolphin. The baby dolphin was injured.

I helped the dolphin, I carried it to the mother. Then the dolphins were happy. There were fishermen coming, the dolphins were in danger. They swam very fast, jumping up and down and diving. The baby dolphin who was called Bubbles, she was very weak, so the fishermen caught her easily. The dolphins didn't realise until they saw that the fisherman caught the baby dolphin.

I quickly swam until it was too late. I got stuck in the net. They pulled me up then I pushed them into the sea. I saw Bubbles then I got the key, but the fishermen grabbed it in rage and anger. I called the dolphins they swam rapidly. They got the baby dolphin and were very happy.

Maariyah Patel (8)
Avon House School, Woodford Green, Essex

HALLOWE'EN

One spooky night there were four children and three adults. The children were called Jack, John and George and the adults Charlotte, David and Harry. David was reading the paper. The Tomson's kid was alive. He said it was Michael Myers.

'There are people dead,' said Harry.
'Also they cut him with a kitchen knife and took his lungs and heart out. The little girl got sliced by the radiator.'
'I'm scared,' said Jack.
'Don't worry, he won't haunt us.'

The next day they went to school. A boy called Tom died. He got stung by a swarm of wasps.
'Oh my goodness,' said Jack. 'Quick, it's class.'
'You are twenty minutes late, where were you three?' said Mr James.

After school they went on the school bus home. Charlotte gave them some tea when they arrived home. Then they watched TV and had dinner then went to bed.

In the morning Jack was dead. There was a hockey stick in his face. His parents were horrified. Micheal Myers had done this.

The criminal Michael Myers was caught.

'Yes!' said the family.

Arjun Saroa (8)
Avon House School, Woodford Green, Essex

THE SQUIRREL'S NUT

Once upon a time there lived a family called the Squirrels. The Squirrels family loved nuts and only would eat nuts.

Every morning the mummy Squirrel would go to the supermarket. But it wasn't just any supermarket, it was a supermarket that only sold nuts. Any nut you could think of in the world and they had it. And it was just for squirrels to go into.

Mummy Squirrel would usually buy economy nuts. Daddy Squirrel would stay with his daughter. On every Friday Daddy would go to work. So when it came to Friday Daddy went to work and Mummy went to the supermarket, and it just the little Squirrel on its own. While she was on her own she found an enormous nut and it was very useful, and so instead of eating it the squirrel wanted to grow it. It was so big the squirrel got stuck in it. When Mummy got home she couldn't find the little squirrel so she rang Daddy and when Daddy came home he shouted out and then he actually found her.

And they were never hungry again.

Spencer Grant (8)
Avon House School, Woodford Green, Essex

A DEADLY SOMETHING

Once upon a time there lived a boy called Bob and he lived in France. His mother and father didn't like France so they left France . . . and came to the best country in the world, England.

Bob believed in ghosts but he didn't believe that there were ghosts in England. They lived in a small hut in the wood. They did not live in a house because they couldn't afford it. They heard that some monster ruled the wood.
Bob just said, 'Ha, there are no monsters in England.' That night Bob woke up in the middle of the night, he heard a howling noise. He looked at his father's bed and all he saw was blood stains leading to the door. The door was wide open, Bob was frightened out of his wits, his heart was pounding. He did not know what it was so he woke his mother up and he said, 'Mum, Mum, Dad is dead!'

So his mother rang the police, and they came straight away, so Bob's mother became a widow. He was very upset because the memories of his father were truly upsetting. After that he decided to go back to France, so his mother took him back to France.

Joshua Martin (9)
Avon House School, Woodford Green, Essex

THE HAUNTED HOUSE

Once upon a time there was a boy named Mitch, he was nineteen, he lived in Australia. It was nice and hot there but he wanted to live in England.

So on his twentieth birthday he got on a plane and he went to live in England. When he arrived he bought a house with some of his birthday money. It looked alright to him, but it wasn't alright. *The house was haunted.* He went into the house and he could smell something in the kitchen and had a look in the fridge. There was all slime in the fridge. Mitch quickly slammed it shut.

He went upstairs to unpack. He went to put some shirts in the cupboard and there were all bugs in the cupboard.

That night he was watching TV and all that was on was people killing other people, so he went to bed. As he pulled back the covers he saw a dead man in his bed, so he got a black sack and threw him out of the window.

The next day Mitch was on the way to the shop. As he was walking there he saw a knife, he picked it up and he said, 'That's strange.' and walked off.

He went into the shop. There where spiderwebs everywhere. He got the newspaper, he paid and went home. There were police all around his house. It wasn't really him who killed the man, it was a vampire. Mitch doesn't know that.
One of the policemen said, 'Check him to see if he has a weapon.'
'Yes, I have found a head and a knife.'
So the police arrested him and he was sent to prison.

Harry Lee (8)
Avon House School, Woodford Green, Essex

CHRISTMAS

On the day before Christmas a little boy called John was very happy. When it came to Christmas he didn't just get presents, but he got to see his family. This little boy had no father, his father died last Christmas and so all he had was his mum and he never got to see his family much. He was an only child and so this was a treat for him to be with his family

The next day his family came round. They opened their presents and then had a lovely turkey for lunch. Then it started to snow. They found a pub and so John and his cousins got to play with the snow. They threw snowballs and then they went home and had dinner and went to bed.

The next morning they all had beans on toast for breakfast and then he had a present from his friends. His friends stayed round the next day and so he had a happy Christmas.

Daisy Pithers (9)
Avon House School, Woodford Green, Essex

THE GHOST HOUSE

Many years ago there was a ghost house. They say who dares to enter never comes out. Fifty-four years ago my grandpa's friend went in and never returned. They say that there are ogres, vampires and other dreadful things in there.

So off I went to the ghost house. First I went into the dark forest and bumped into an ogre. I found a sword and killed the ogre. I was walking with the sword in my hand and suddenly I heard something roar.

It was a fire-breathing dragon. He nearly got me with his flame but I escaped. I threw my sword in his stomach and killed him.

Then I came to a city, I was suspicious, it was so very quiet and still, nothing moved. Bodies lay on the floor. I was walking along the path and I came to the ghost house! I opened the door, it was creepy, it was giving me the heebee-jeebies. I walked in and heard a ghost voice.

Then there was a graveyard. Suddenly there was a voice. It was a zombie's! He said, 'David, get out of here.'
I ran out of the ghost house, and never returned.

David Nagler (8)
Avon House School, Woodford Green, Essex

SCHOOL'S FINISHED

There're these girls in the last class of school and there names are Elizabeth, Radhika, Maarijah, Kelly, Daisy and Rebekah. There are some cool boys too but not many people know them.

It was nearly the end of the year and the children were doing SATs tests. The next day the teacher read out the marks. She said the girls' marks first. She said, 'Elizabeth 30/30,' when she said the girls' marks, it was always 30/30.

The teachers are kind to everyone except for children that are naughty and when teachers get cross you know what they look like, they have big, large heads that go red.

Then it was time to go home, so they went home.

The next day was Saturday and it was Maariyah's birthday, so all the girls went to her party. They played a long time. All the girls slept over too.

Then it was Monday, and it was the last day of school. It was good, all the girls were going to the same secondary school. Then everyone way saying goodbye to the teacher.
Then the girls went home saying, 'School's finished.'

Kelly De Freitas (8)
Avon House School, Woodford Green, Essex

TIME'S REVENGE

It was a cold, misty night. The bite of fresh air in Nick's lungs made him shiver. He was about fifteen, a tall, lean boy with a navy blue winter coat wrapped tightly around him.

As he neared the small, comfortable bungalow that was his home, he heard a rustle from the forest. It was on the far side of his school, and had a shortcut to his house. It was named after Edward Green, the missing explorer. There was another shuffling from the dark and cold wood, this time it was louder. He desperately wanted to explore, to see what was making that strange noise but his mother had forbidden him to enter it, for some reason that she wouldn't explain. Most people knew the secret, and it aggravated him so much that he was one of the only people who didn't know.

He looked around, checking to make sure that no one from school was down that street. He pulled up his collar and shifted his bag further up his back to stop people from recognising him. After checking the street once again, he started into Green Forest.

It was dark and creepy. Once he had gone in, Nick wished he hadn't. There were cobwebs everywhere. Nick stopped at a particular one near a big oak tree. It had a silver sphere glowing . . . *wham!* In front of him, there was a huge wormhole.
'I am time. The Earth people treat me like I am not real! They will pay!'
In a flash, Nick was gone.

Matthew Davies (10)
Hamstel County Junior School, Southend-on-Sea, Essex

A DAY IN THE LIFE OF MOLLY

I saw Molly walking to school with Abbie. Molly was the most popular girl in school. I wondered what it would be like to be Molly for a day. After school, I walked home and saw my house ahead. I ran to it. I opened the door and saw my mum cooking dinner for her and Dad. The scent of sausages and chips whipped up my nose. I went up to my room to do a heap of homework that Mrs Study had given me. At eight o'clock I finally finished. I looked out of my window and wished I was like Molly again when I saw a star. 'Isn't that beautiful,' I said.
I tucked myself into bed and went to sleep.

The next morning I woke up and looked in the mirror like I normally did and had a great shock. I was Molly! I had good looks, no geeky glasses and infact, no geeky features at all. I looked around my unusually large bedroom to find that the whole house had changed! I then went out of my room and downstairs to find a cat sitting on the chair in the hallway by the door. I haven't got a cat. But in this case I had. I had heard that Molly had one, that meant I had one as well. I walked into the kitchen to find that my parents had changed as well, but not in appearance.
'You are ten seconds late for breakfast young lady. That means you must go to bed ten seconds earlier than last night,' snapped my dad in his I'm so mad with you tone of voice.
'Sorry,' I said sarcastically.
I ate my breakfast quickly in order to get away from Mum and Dad. I put on my clothes and went out the door ready to go to school when I saw someone at the gate. Abbie.
'Come on Molly.'

Abbie was a tall sixth grader, a fashion queen and Molly's best friend so I thought it best to walk to school with her. As we walked, all Abbie did was chat, chat, chat.
Why can't she shut up, she's getting really annoying I thought.

Finally we got to school in which, by that time, Abbie had shut up. Abbie went into class. I looked around to see if the real Molly was there. She wasn't. I went into my classroom. We had a double dose of history and an extra helping of jealousy. I had never realised how many people were jealous of Molly and her intelligence and good looks. Whenever I walked past someone, they sneered at me. I didn't like it one bit. I wondered how Molly could cope with all the jealousy. I walked home after school without Abbie as I had learnt my lesson from this morning and had got a headache not only from her but from the teachers telling me off for wearing a mingy necklace to school.

When I got home, which was pretty early because I had no clubs, I ran upstairs to look at myself in the mirror.
'I don't want to be Molly anymore. I do not like people being horrible to me. It's not very nice.'
I heard Mum come in. Dad wasn't with her. He was doing a late shift tonight at the office and wouldn't be back until late. I went to bed without anything to eat as I was too tired to do anything. At eight o'clock I fell asleep.

The next morning I woke up in Molly's house again! I didn't look in the mirror or have any breakfast. I went straight to school. Abbie wasn't waiting by the gate for me (or should I say Molly).
I was shocked. Maybe she is ill or something, I thought.

I walked to school on my own when people seemed to sneer at me but not in the way they did the day before. I of course ignored this and went into my classroom. At break time, I went to the toilets to wash my hands, because we had just had chemistry, when I looked in the mirror and saw a sight that really pleased me. I was me!

When I went home, I saw that Mum was back to normal and so was Dad and the house. I was so pleased. After this experience, I will never wish to be anyone or wish for anything again!

Chelsi Pinkerton-Jarvis (11)
Hamstel County Junior School, Southend-on-Sea, Essex

GRANDMA ANNA

It was Hallowe'en in the year 2000. Amy, her mum and grandad were describing the scariest part of their lives so far. Grandad said for him it was when Grandma died. Kate, Amy's mum, ran out of the room crying. 'Don't talk about Mum!' she cried.

Amy went to bed, she hated seeing her mum cry. Amy got into bed. Then a voice echoed around the room. It was calling Amy's name. Amy screamed! It was the ghost of Grandma Anna. 'Amy, don't worry it's me,' she called.

Amy breathed heavily. Grandma Anna tried to calm her down as much as possible but Amy just got more scared. Suddenly without warning, more ghosts came in. They all tried to strangle Amy, but Grandma Anna just told them to go away because this was her granddaughter. So they all went to haunt another house.

Amy tried not to breathe so loudly but it was no use. Grandma Anna asked where Grandad was, so Amy pointed, with a shaking hand, downstairs. Grandma Anna and Amy went downstairs.
'Look Grandad, it's Grandma!' Amy called.
'Oh, ha, ha, another Hallowe'en joke.' he answered.
Grandma quickly told Amy this, 'Didn't I tell you? You and *you* only can see ghosts!'

Emma Thwaites (10)
Heatherton House School, Amersham, Bucks

THE BARN

A man, named George Frederick Wayford, had died in 1936 at the age of eighty-seven. Nobody knew how he had passed away - but they knew where . . .

Up in Scotland in Apple Tree Farm there lived a young girl named Emerald Wayford with her mother and father. It was nearly Christmas. I know most people look forward to Christmas but Emerald didn't, for at Christmas she would smell smoke and start choking.

One night she lay in bed shaking and heard a tapping sound at the window. She knew it had just begun. Soon she smelt smoke and then came the choking. She lay in bed, only breathing through gasping sobs, then staggered out of bed making her way towards the window. She flung it open and gulped down the night's fresh air . . .

The following winter's day, playing down near the old barn, she heard a creaking coming from it. Having never been in the barn she stepped nervously towards it. Emerald let out a gasp as she saw what was there - a ghostly figure in ragged robes. In a split second he was gone, Emerald started spinning, she saw fire, heard voices and collapsed on the barn floor . . .

Zoe Hunt (9)
Heatherton House School, Amersham, Bucks

THE MYSTERIOUS SKATEBOARD

Lottie, Grace, George and Bossy the dog were keen skateboarders. Unfortunately, George wasn't very good.

One day, George found a very old skateboard in his shed. He threw it on the ground. Bossy jumped onto the skateboard and started to do some tricks. George pushed the dog off the board, and jumped on. George started performing difficult tricks. He could not believe that he was so good.

George and Bossy ran to the skateboard park where their friends were. Lottie and Grace shouted, 'Hi,' but George ignored them. He jumped onto the board and started difficult tricks. His friends could not believe their eyes. 'How did you do that? Who's been teaching you?' asked Lottie.

George told his friends how he had found the skateboard. He jumped back on, but this time the board took off out of control. George shouted for help, but he was going too fast. The board went up the ramp, and over the top. George flew off and crashed into a brick wall. They rushed him to hospital.

Later his mother came to see him and explained that the board had belonged to his great uncle who had died while performing on the very skateboard George had found!

Charlotte Lowe (9)
Heatherton House School, Amersham, Bucks

NEVER TO RETURN

I entered, shaking but excited. I switched on my torch. Now I could see instead of being shrouded in darkness.

Redgrave Station was built of red brick. Lichen covered the damp areas. A musty and damp smell hung in the air. Slipping on the wet, puddle-filled floor I noticed old clothes bags. In 1914 people would seek shelter from the noise and bombing outside. They'd lie on the hard, wet platform. People snoring, moving about. I could imagine it.

Cooing pigeons flew over my head. Rain drummed on the roof above. Then I saw something.

I nervously walked forward, like a cat sneaking past a sleeping dog, unaware of who was behind me. I shivered all over and suddenly felt cold. My heart started beating. I turned around . . . 'Aaaaaah!'

A clear person in rags stood behind me, confused and delirious. Black marks covered his face. He shivered. Tripping over my untied shoelaces, I fell onto the railway lines.

Suddenly the railway started to vibrate, the walls shook. I tried to haul myself up, but I was too weak. A huge, clear object was coming nearer and nearer. The train was approaching . . .

And there I lay, on the track . . . helpless . . . waiting.

Charlotte Webber (11)
Heatherton House School, Amersham, Bucks

NIGHTMARE AT MIDNIGHT

Katie was lying in bed tossing and turning under the duvet trying to get to sleep. She had watched a horror movie and she was scared that the ghost in the movie was real. The clock in the hall struck twelve, then Katie heard the creaking noise up and down the hall. Then it went down the stairs and something went outside and carefully shut the door behind it.

Katie couldn't stop herself, she went outside and followed the sound that gravel makes when you walk on it. Suddenly she stopped. Standing right in front of her was a ghost carrying a knife in its hand. The ghost just carried on walking and it went straight to the park that Katie went to everyday after school. Katie heard another creak, except this time it came from a swing.

On the swing was another ghost, a child ghost. Suddenly the ghost carrying the knife went up to the ghost on the swing and started stabbing it in the neck. Katie then realised that this was exactly the same story as the one she had watched on the TV, except this was real life! This was Katie's nightmare at midnight!

Grace Pickard (10)
Heatherton House School, Amersham, Bucks

WHAT LURKED IN THE SHADOWS?

In a dark and desolate underground station lived an old, old feeble man dressed in rags and wrapped tightly in torn yellow blankets. This tramp's name was Freddy, Freddy Crayson. On the smelly, dirty platform Freddy had put out in front of him, an old cap which he no longer wore and in this cap lay just a few copper pennies. Sitting patiently beside Freddy was Freddy's beloved dog, a brown Labrador, Rusty.

Life was much the same everyday. Freddy and Rusty just sat, staring at hordes of bustling people piling into the underground station at all different times of what seemed like everlasting days.

Until, one night. Freddy, for some reason couldn't go to sleep. He was hearing bizarre noises. From out of the darkness, lurking in the shadows stood something or someone. Freddy grew more and more frightened. He trembled with fear and a chill ran up his spine. Terrified as he was, Freddy was longing to see who was there.

Eventually, Freddy summoned up his courage to reveal the mystery of who awaited there. Nobody could call him a coward, but now, as Freddy approached, his heart began to beat as fast as the milliseconds on a stopwatch would go . . .

Lara Stephenson (11)
Heatherton House School, Amersham, Bucks

THE GHOSTLY FIGURE

'We are afraid to hear that Duncan Goodhew was killed last night at Millfield School's swimming pool.' My dad read the atrocious news from the paper aloud. 'Police say that he was beaten up and thrown into the pool to drown, we have not yet found who is responsible for the murder.' Dad dropped the paper and slowly took off his old-fashioned glasses . . .

There I was, standing on the side ready to dive into the pool Duncan had drowned in. As I climbed onto the diving board a chill ran up my back and my knees felt weak, the water rippled and . . . *bang!* the gunshot went. As I approached the other side, worried about my tumble turn there was a loud shriek which came from the toilets. I stopped swimming. There with my two eyes I saw a black ghostly figure run swiftly out of the door leading to the car park. As the audience ran to the toilets I jumped out of the pool, shivering I grabbed my towel and ran rapidly outside.

The figure was nowhere to be seen, but behind me I could feel some deep breathing. Thinking it was my dad I turned around . . . but I was wrong.

Daniella Peña (11)
Heatherton House School, Amersham, Bucks

THE PERFECT MURDER

If you asked anybody about Shepley Outdoor Pool, they would reply, 'Nice place to take kids during summer.' But none of them knew the chilling events that had taken place there . . .

Jenny stared at the wrought iron gates in front of her and took a deep breath. For an extrovert a midnight swim should not have been exceptionally daring, but tonight was different. After being upset by friends she had come for a swim to get it out of her system. She had an ambition to be an Olympic swimmer and trained regularly. With no sound she slid gently into the pool.

After a few lengths, Jenny's thoughts turned to toddler Jordan Lewis' murder. He had been smothered using a blue towel. She shuddered to think about it. She suddenly began to hear slight footsteps. Stop it, she thought to herself. The footsteps continued as she clambered out. A tall, cloaked figure approached her through the mist.

Jenny felt a chill in her veins. To her horror, staring down at her was a woman's face, filled with malice and evil determination. 'I did it!' she whispered, in a chilling tone. And, as she turned and walked away, a blue towel fell to the floor.

Laura Valdez (10)
Heatherton House School, Amersham, Bucks

THE TRAIN DRIVER AMONG THE DEAD

It all started when Frederick and Mrs Lockport went to the first ever Lee Common funfair. Now Mrs Lockport looked like Geri Halliwell and the worst punk of the century. As expected, someone with a cactus-like hairstyle would abandon her fledgling.

Alone, Fred looked around to find the ghost train completely deserted. As soon as he got on he realised something was wrong. It was only then that he noticed a shadowy figure. Fred slowly moved from carriage to carriage till he got to the figure. As he tapped him, voices slowly started to rise within him saying, 'Tim, Tim, catch the boy' and 'Don't go after him!' Fred's blood froze as the figure turned round and empty sockets met his own eyes, before disappearing.

'Hey sonny, wake up,' came a voice ringing in his ear.
'What?' said Fred sitting up to find himself staring at a red-faced clown.
'You must have taken quite a fall,' replied the clown.
'Do you remember anything?'
'I remember the ghost train,' said Fred.
'You must have bumped your head, because we haven't had a ghost train since young Tim was killed jumping off the train to save a child.'

Emma Price (9)
Heatherton House School, Amersham, Bucks

SUSPICION

It was a cold, misty day and Lucy Brown was going to buy some meat as her mum had asked. The shop was very old and musty. There was no one there so the lights were turned off.

Suddenly Lucy felt a tight squeezing round her bony neck. There was someone tightening a rope round her neck. Lucy was struggling to stop the murderer. She gave up. He had beaten her. No one knew who had done it. The only thing they knew was Lucy had died a horrible death. The shop had been closed down in case the murderer was waiting for another victim.

A few days later it was the funeral. Lucy's mum was terribly distressed. She was late. As she passed through the graveyard, there was a whisper. She turned round. There was no one there. Then she heard a creak. There was someone behind her. She tried to turn round, she couldn't, it was the murderer. He had come back for more.

Lucy's mum's last words were, 'Always beware, don't leave your house, suspicion is everywhere you go!'
So everyone, remember suspicion is everywhere, suspicion is your worst nightmare!

Rachel Raffety (10)
Heatherton House School, Amersham, Bucks

ANDELBEER HALL

Andelbeer Hall was well known for it was owned by a very famous family that lived there. When the Andelbeers' daughter was murdered they fled, leaving the house unattended to.

Later people visited the house and when they were shown round they told their children to go and play in the garden. They didn't come back for hours.
'Where have you been?' their parents demanded.
'In the garden, playing with a girl.'
Their parents were confused. What girl they thought.

Years after the Andelbeers left, a family called the Johnsons bought the house and a wrinkled lady showed them round. The Johnsons were a family of three. A mother, father and a daughter Roberta. When the mother was little she had been to the hall. 'I came here when I was little.' she said.

Roberta was getting bored. 'Go into the garden,' her father said.
In the garden the child saw the ghost. She had black hair and a white petticoat. Roberta went into the garden and saw a girl in the window. She had a white shirt and jeans like her.
'Are you hot?' said the girl.
'Why, should I be?'
'Well you have black hair and a white petticoat so I thought you would be.' And then she vanished.

Emma Palios (10)
Heatherton House School, Amersham, Bucks

THE STEAK KNIFE

Helen lay in bed, listening to the RAF bombers flying to Germany. The year was 1942. Her home, Nickelwell Farm, was silent. It had been built by her great grandad, Edward Phipps and had been handed down through generations.

She was just dozing off when she heard a shrill scream. Slowly she pulled on her dressing gown and tiptoed into her parents' room. She saw the bed, with two breathing lumps. She then tiptoed into the bathroom, and saw water in the bath. She reached down to pull the plug. That's funny, she thought, the water's warm. Then she tiptoed back to bed.

The next morning she was about to sit down in the bath when she saw something glinting in the water. She pulled it out. It was her dad's steak knife! Quickly she ran downstairs shouting, 'Mam! I've found Dad's steak knife!'
'What are you doing with that steak knife? I'm surprised you haven't cut yourself!'
'But Mam . . .'

That evening Helen had her bath as usual. As she dried herself, she heard a faint moaning sound. She stopped and listened. She saw a white figure walk through the wall. It was carrying, dripping with blood . . . a steak knife.

Sara Anderson (11)
Heatherton House School, Amersham, Bucks

KRYPTONITE

No one knew how Ben Luther died, but I do, because I killed him. Ben lived on his own, his parents had separated when he was younger. Him and his dad had never seen his mother since. He lived on his own near the New Forest. It seemed a normal place, but it had never been the same after Ben's death.

He was on the A39, when he suddenly saw a deer crossing the road. He swerved madly to the side, his heart thumping. He hit a tree and what he thought was a shard of glass (but was really kryptonite) fell though the open-top roof and stuck itself in his hand. He tried to pull it out, but it was imbedded in his skin, piercing him like a dagger. He phoned up Antony, his friend, and he agreed to pick Ben up from where he had crashed. He picked Ben up and dropped him home.

When he got home he went to bed and tried to sleep, but he couldn't. He kept hearing footsteps coming up the stairs, and knocking on the door, but when he opened it there was no one there. Some ask why I killed him, but the truth is, he killed my family. It's justice . . .

Emily Corden (10)
Heatherton House School, Amersham, Bucks

A UNRETURNED VISIT

It was just an ordinary evening at 11 Bridlington Spur. The weather was just the same but with a flaming red sun and not a cloud in the sky as the sun sank beneath the quiet town's rooftops.

Roxanne Seaton was having a fun sleepover with her best friend Michelle Cooper. At night, when all the family were asleep, hushed voices came from Roxanne's room.
'Do you know that girl on TV? She was kidnapped by a ghost.' said Roxanne.
'Don't be daft, I mean, they're not real,' said Michelle, as she dropped her earring on the floor.
As she bent down to get it, Roxanne said in a mysterious voice, 'Unless we find out . . . Michelle turn off the light and close the door!'
'What? Are you serious?' said Michelle in a worried voice (but she did it anyway). The room was pitch-black now. Roxanne stood up, her body just visible in the darkness. Roxanne looked into the mirror and said these very words, 'The candyman, the candyman, the candyman.'
A huge figure stepped across the room. Roxanne screamed deafeningly.

The next morning Michelle looked around the room, blood was on the carpet of the room but . . . Roxanne never returned!

Rosanna Dolling (11)
Heatherton House School, Amersham, Bucks

THE GHOST OF PRINSTON MANOR

I am going to tell a story which happened to me when I was twelve years old. It was true. It really happened to me.

I was moving into Prinston Manor where my uncle lived until he died. He left us this house in his will but no one knew he would die so soon. Police said it was a heart attack, but no one knew the truth.

As we unlocked the door I felt a strange vibe as I stepped in. It didn't take long for us to settle in. But before I went to sleep I heard a terrifying scream come from downstairs. I rushed down but all there was left was a long grey coat.

For our school project we had to do a piece of writing about our house. As I was researching the history of Prinston Manor I found out horrifying news. A man had murdered a maid years ago. They never found the murderer, but the maid haunts the house.

It took ages for me to tell, but when I did it was too late. That evening my father was murdered by a ghost. He murdered my uncle and now my father. The ghost is here, in our house.

Rosie Webber (10)
Heatherton House School, Amersham, Bucks

THE TUNNEL OF DOOM

'Jodie will you take some chocolates for Granny because it's her birthday today. You should take Liam with you as well.'

Jodie and Liam set off and took the bus to Avenue Lane. But a disaster happened when they walked to the next station and the town became flooded.

Liam decided that they would have to go through the dangerous tunnel for it was the only way. Everyone was talking about them and that they were so brave, some people couldn't believe it.

Jodie and Liam were really quite unsure, Jodie and Liam took a few steps. With every step their heart beat faster. Liam followed slowly behind Jodie. He said to Jodie, 'Do you hear that.' Jodie didn't answer.

Suddenly some bloodsucking bats came out and started flapping their wings. Some sucked and some flew away.

Jodie and Liam were relieved when they'd gone but not for long, something was still there. Liam nearly started crying so he held on to Jodie's arm. Out of the dark a second later came a strange figure with bright green eyes and brown fuzzy hair. Jodie thought it must be ghost!

Anna Court (10)
Heatherton House School, Amersham, Bucks

FEAR OF THE UNKNOWN

Stacey and her parents had just moved into what used to be an old Victorian orphanage. In the bedroom, where Stacey was just unpacking her belongings, she noticed that her mirror had moved. She went to move it back and saw the reflection of a small Victorian girl standing behind her and crying out for help. She saw a Victorian man trying to drag the girl away into the darkness. She turned to help the girl but they had gone. The next day she was on alert for spooky things. She asked her mother about the house, which is when she found out its history.

Later, when Stacey was combing her hair, she noticed there was a piece of the mirror missing. She didn't know why but she was drawn to find the missing piece. She explored the house. In a small attic room, lined with mirrors, she found a box, and she was sure the missing piece was inside. It was!

Running back to her room she slotted the piece of mirror back into its place. For a second she thought she saw the girl again, smiling and waving. There was a gust of wind and she knew she had set the spirits free.

Rachel Douglas (10)
Heatherton House School, Amersham, Bucks

KRINGCLETON COTTAGE

Rosie Kidington was one who was ordinary in every way but something was not as seemed. She lived in an ordinary cottage with an ordinary dog Spot. Rosie did not live alone in the cottage but with her mum Anne. The cottage was a creamy yellow with roses growing round the windows in vines.

But Rosie was growing suspicious since on every 23rd April she had seen a figure walking across the hall. Today was the 22nd and tomorrow would be Friday and that means this time she would be at school. Just the thought of it was daunting.

So, the next day Rosie went to school with no idea what would happen. And when she arrived at school she took out her pencil case for English. She saw a ghostly figure reflected on her ruler. Rosie just ignored this and carried on with the rest of the day, thinking her mind was playing tricks on her.

That night Rosie found some old papers behind her closet and started reading them. They were the family tree. Curious to see where Rosie was on the tree she found her name but next to it a piece of paper was covering something so she ripped off the paper to find she had a twin sister tormenting her!

Emma Evans (10)
Heatherton House School, Amersham, Bucks

MURDER AT BUCKHOLT MANOR

Tom arrived back from work. The car went through the heavy metal gates, making the stones in the drive grind together.

He looked for his wife, Rachel, in the house but she was nowhere to be seen. Tom thought to himself and finally came to a conclusion . . . the *garden!*

He was checking the garden, when suddenly, to his horror, he saw his wife Rachel tied to a tree with a rope around her soft neck, tight! She was dead.

Tom didn't waste another minute . . . he rushed to his car, jumped in and drove to the Riverton police station. He told the policeman what had happened, not totally sure himself, but boy was that a bad idea.

The very next day he was locked up for the murder of Rachel Dennings!

In Tom's rusty cell, where rats nibbled at his feet in search of food, Tom was eager for revenge.

On visiting day, he waited impatiently for a visitor. When he came, he was a man in a long black cloak, with a hood covering his face.
'Who are you?' Tom asked, quivering,
But the man only answered, 'Why don't you just call me your worst nightmare!'

Lucy Panter (10)
Heatherton House School, Amersham, Bucks

THE GLOWING FIGURE

Amyina Wendy was a young, curious and imaginative girl. She lived in an old Victorian house that was quite ordinary to say the least, until one day, not too long ago, something strange happened.

It was in the middle of the night and she woke from the continuous noise of people mocking her barking dog, but she didn't mind because she knew, (or thought anyway) that it was some stupid teenagers with nothing better to do at midnight. Then suddenly, changing her thoughts entirely, she heard a creaking on the stairs.

Amyina, becoming very suspicious, crept silently out of bed to go and see, but nothing was there. She felt a hand on her shoulder and a sudden surge of horror struck her. She turned around only to see her father asking why she was awake. She returned to bed.

Later, she awoke once more to hear more creaking and shouting, but this time she went downstairs and into the kitchen where someone with ice-cold hands, grabbed her around the neck, 'Dad, stop, this isn't funny,' she struggled to say, nearly suffocating. But when she managed to turn around a glowing figure stood there with a knife and . . .

Victoria Mears (10)
Heatherton House School, Amersham, Bucks

WHY MURDER HER?

Chilsley Public School was seemingly pleasant, happy and content. Everyday the laughter was stopped . . . and poised pencils at the ready hit the blank, lined pages, as soon as the copper bell sounded. They stood innocently silent and unaware.

Laura O'Neil in one of the upper classes was left in the huge building unattended, hesitantly waiting for her mum, as school was finished now. She thought it was a perfect opportunity to complete her homework. The caretaker was left to supervise Laura but had done nothing with the responsibility and Laura was growing worried.

Sitting at the front single desk with only a carefully balanced sidelight on, it began to flicker between brightness and the faint sound of her pencil scribbling was the only noise she could hear.

Suddenly she caught a glimpse of the door closing and turned around frantically but nothing could be seen. Her eyes slowly focused back on her work. She stared out of the dark window and watched the raindrops chasing each other down the windowpane. Then she recognised the creak from behind her chair. The grip from her pencil loosened as she turned around. Her pencil descended to her desk. Something pierced her neck.

Silence . . .

Rosalynn Youdan
Heatherton House School, Amersham, Bucks

THE DOLL

Sally jumped out of bed screaming, 'It's my birthday.' For she had remembered that her father was taking her to the old toyshop.

Later, she jumped in the car with her dad. When she reached the shop she climbed out. When inside the musty shop Sally chose a red-eyed doll. Her father tried to reason with her but Sally was insistent so he gave in and bought it.

When she got home Sally's dad said, 'When you've finished put it back in the box.' Despite his instructions Sally left her box in the cheerful living room.

Just as Sally was getting to sleep she heard a haunting voice, 'Sally, I'm on the first step.' The voice went on to twenty-seven steps. 'Sally, I'm in your bedroom, Sally I'm going to kill you!'

Next morning, Sally's dad knocked on her door and said cheerfully, 'Good morning.' Strange. He knocked again, 'Are you there?' Silence. He went in, and saw bloodstained sheets but no Sally, he turned, he saw the doll with eyes gleaming.

He ran downstairs to call the police. As he pressed the keypad of the phone under the mirror, he saw the doll's reflection. Terrified, he ran to the door.

Hannah Maguire (11)
Heatherton House School, Amersham, Bucks

THE VOICE

It all started with an exciting Brownie meeting. Anya, the leader had organised a meeting to a graveyard to see if they could find Zoe's grandad's grave for a Brownie badge. They were sitting down in a ring, toasting marshmallows and drinking hot chocolate. Zoe's mum had to collect her early because she had a performance of 'Jack' at school the next day.

Zoe lay down in her bed and started to read, when she heard a chilling voice saying spookily, 'Zoe, I'm at your front door . . . Zoe, I'm at the bottom of the stairs . . . Zoe, I'm at the top of the stairs . . . Zoe, I'm at your bedroom door . . . Zoe, I've opened your door . . . Zoe, I'm coming to get you.'

She sat up, sweat was running down her face, thank goodness it was all a dream . . . or was it? She saw a smoky, white figure before her room began to black out. Her head was spinning, all she could see was a blinding white light around her . . . she felt a pain in her stomach, she drew her terminal breath . . . before a wave of darkness swept over her.

Alexandra Reynolds (11)
Heatherton House School, Amersham, Bucks

BE WARNED

It was a horrible morning and Ali Jonson awoke early, today she was going to see a film at the London Thames cinema with her friend Holly Smith.

As they approached the cinema they saw that there was a plaque, it was devoted to a girl who died there exactly ten years ago. It read *In memory of Mandy Willows, age 13.*
'She was the same age as us,' said Holly.
'Yes . . . creepy,' replied Ali.

In the middle of the movie it was extremely scary and Ali gripped the chair with fright. Then she felt a thumping on the back of her chair, she turned around but nobody was there. But scratched into the chair were two words . . . *'Be warned!'*
Ali turned back around and tapped Holly on the shoulder.
'Holly, Holly, look at the chair behind us.' They turned around to look but there was nothing there.

As they walked out at the end of the movie she saw a hooded figure, she approached it cautiously. There was something wrong with the figure, it didn't feel right. There was something dripping from its cloak. (Could it be blood?). Thoughts came racing to her head, from the plaque to the chair to the hooded figure, she ran.

Liza Hart (11)
Heatherton House School, Amersham, Bucks

THE BRIDGE

Charlotte stepped into the empty carriage and opened her magazine. She was visiting her grandpa who lived in Dorton, a delightful, small village.

Charlotte looked up to see a girl of about ten, wearing hippy clothes, had entered the carriage.
'Hello,' said the girl, 'my name is Sarah.'
'Hello, I'm Charlotte, nice to meet you.'

During the journey Charlotte and Sarah got on well. Apparently Sarah lived in Dorton and attended the local school.

It was nearly four-thirty when they arrived. Charlotte set off towards the bridge into the village, but Sarah called to her, 'I know a prettier way, follow me.' Sarah was right, the route had beautiful scenery and was much more fun, even though it was longer.

Charlotte's Grandpa was happy to see her, but puzzled when she mentioned Sarah. He thought he knew all the children in the village.

Next morning, Charlotte went to collect the local newspaper. The front page stated that at four-thirty the previous evening, Dorton Bridge had collapsed, fortunately nobody was injured. The article went on to say that forty years ago to the day, young Sarah Morton from the village had tragically fallen to her death from the bridge.

Catherine Sutton (11)
Heatherton House School, Amersham, Bucks

THE SKULKING FIGURE

Brring brring, the telephone rang, startling Jenny. She jumped abruptly, and picked up the phone. 'Hello?' she answered, politely.

'Hi Jen, it's Liz, I've got to go, but you need to meet me at midnight at school. We have to check our reports to see if they say we've been in mischief. My dad won't let me go on holiday with you if my report is bad. They come home next week.'

'Okay,' Jen replied. 'I'll meet you there tonight.'

That night, the two girls met at the entrance. Liz slunk silently into school, Jen following uneasily behind. Once they had found their reports, they flicked through them, searching, panic-stricken, for their records. Then they heard it. A creaking, groaning sound of a door. Jenny froze. Liz's hand jerked in shock, sending her report floating to the floor.

Suddenly, a small creak came from the door and to their horror, they saw a figure lurking towards them as they backed into the darkness. The figure skulked forwards, lunging at them. They hit out at it, but their hands just swiped thin air. So . . . so that meant that . . . it was a . . . a . . . it couldn't be a . . . ghost?

Annabel Poor (11)
Heatherton House School, Amersham, Bucks

SASHA AND THE GHOSTS

The sun set and all went dark. Sasha and Laura were camping out. It was midnight and Sasha was awake, suspicious about what was going on outside her red and green tent that her father put up earlier in the day.

Sasha peered outside the tent. She heard the wind whistle through the trees and the owls hoot. She heard the swooping of the bats and saw the shadows of the spiders. She crept out, leaving Laura and the tent behind. She was walking round in circles. There was a pond on her left. She saw the ripples of the leaves as they hit the clear, shimmering water one by one. She saw dragons and ghosts on the red and orange bricks of the walls.

It seemed miles from the house. Sasha could see the navy blue sky with little white dots which were stars. Thunder crackled from the sky and rain fell. The stars disappeared and grey clouds raced across the dark sky . . . the rain changed from pouring to drizzle and then to nothing at all.

The shadows began once more, monsters and really creepy creatures. Sasha took one last look around and fell to the ground in shock.

Emily Ceurvorst (10)
Heatherton House School, Amersham, Bucks

No Parents

There were four girls called Rachel, Nicola, Katie and Sneha. They were in Y5 Whitlow and they were good friends.

There was a competition on at school for who could write the best story and bake the best cake. Whoever won would choose two holiday places to go to without their parents. Nearly everyone entered.

It was the day the winners were revealed. Miss Nicholson said, 'The winners are Katie, Sneha, Nicola and Rachel.'
'Ahhh!' The winners screamed and screamed.
Everyone clapped but they were a bit upset because they didn't win.
Miss Nicholson said, 'What resorts do you choose?'
Katie, Sneha, Nicola and Rachel gathered round talking and then said, 'Hawaii and Paris.'

They all went home, packed for Hawaii. They went for three weeks. They laid on the beach and swam. They came back to London with a lovely tan, stayed for the weekend and then went to Paris. They did lots of shopping and came back to London with bags and bags of clothes.

They were happy to be back because they missed their friends, teachers and especially their family.

Rachel Kelly (9)
John Bramston Primary School, Ilford, Essex

AFTER THE RACE!

'Hey Harry, thanks so much for your help. My dad was going to put me in the Army! He said I was lazy and just sat and watched TV, but now after the race, he was boasting to all his mates about me. Thanks alot, I owe you one pal.'
'No problem Terry. Did you see how I almost caught you up in the end? Nice touch wasn't it?'
'That was great. My dad was so excited that he even rang up my mum at the hairdressers. Thanks a lot Harry.'

And with that the tortoise and the hare shook hands and walked off, laughing till they cried.

Hannah De Souza (8)
John Bramston Primary School, Ilford, Essex

THE GREAT CHASE!

The brown blur was getting closer and closer. I could almost feel it breathing on the back of my neck. I glanced back. Its fangs glistening in the sunlight, its eyes dead, focused on me! What was a blur a few moments ago, was no longer a blur. My legs were getting tired. Any minute now I would drop dead exhausted . . . and surely be eaten alive. My coat was weighing me down, it was drenched in sweat.

I couldn't believe the size of this thing. It probably weighed the amount of two fully grown adults. Its legs were huge. For every two steps I took, it took one, and once again it was right behind me.

In the distance I could faintly see a face. As I got closer I realised it was Jake. My heart leapt for joy. Yes, I thought, I'm saved! That sudden burst of excitement must have done some good because I suddenly shot off like a rocket straight into Jake's arms, safe from that stupid dog. 'Fluffy, there you are!' Jake said stroking my soft brown fur.

Sarah De Souza (11)
John Bramston Primary School, Ilford, Essex

TRAPPED

She was a prisoner, of not only her uncle, but of her own mind as well. All opinions; thoughts, comments, could never be expressed, for the sheer thought of the belt slashing at her back. She longed to have a life, longed to be able to talk for herself, longed to be free of her own mind. She endlessly wished upon a shooting star, and every time that she wished, she wished the same wish over and over again.

Her uncle was a cruel, hard-hearted man, whose soul had disappeared a long time ago. All of his spite and jealousy, though nothing to do with her, was taken out on her.

Though had he have known that she was to break free of his grasp, he'd have slashed her with the belt a million times harder.

Daisy Keens (11)
John Bramston Primary School, Ilford, Essex

THE HAUNTED CHURCH

One stuffy, hot afternoon Susan, Mell and Sarah were preparing for their trip to the haunted church.

'Do you think we'll need some rope?' asked Sarah.

'OK, we'll take the rope - just in case you fall off the tower again!'

'Hey, that's not funny!' and Sarah threw a cushion at Mell.

'Stop that, it won't solve anything,' shouted Susan. The two girls froze, 'That's better! Now we want to be prepared for anything.'

'So that includes if Mell needs to put on more make-up?' joked Sarah.

Mell's face turned bright red. *'Sarah!'*

'Sorry,' said Sarah.

'Thank you.'

Meanwhile, in the kitchen, Susan's mother was having second thoughts about the girls going. Too late - the girls were already at the graveyard.

'Sarah, you go first . . .' said Mell.

'Why should I?' replied Sarah.

'Because you're the bravest out of us all,' Mell exclaimed.

So Sarah crept inside the church and was immediately met by a ghost.

'Arrgghh!' Sarah screamed and rushed deeper inside the church.

'Was that Sarah?' whispered Susan.

'I think so,' Mell answered.

'Let's go and find her,' they said together.

Someone tapped Mell's back. Mell span around and came face to face with a headless ghost. Meanwhile, Sarah ran into an army of ghosts and zombies caught her and flung her in a hanging cage.

Back with the other two, they had found some benches and laid down for the night. All through the night they were bumped by ghosts.

In the morning the police found Susan and Mell, but they never saw Sarah again . . .

Heather Musgrave (8)
Little Gaddesden Primary School, Little Gaddesden, Herts

THE HAUNTED COTTAGE

Fiona was a small, kind girl with very long blonde hair. She was about nine years old. She was well behaved and spoilt, but she was very grateful for her spoiltness. She lived in a huge posh house with millions of servants. She was an only child and had a room of her own. In her room there was a big four-poster bed with cream sheets and pillowcases.

One day, when she was alone in the big house, she decided to go for an adventure. So she got out her biggest bag and packed a box of matches, a rug, a magnifying glass, some binoculars, a sports bottle with strawberry juice in, a packet of marshmallows, her mum's kitchen knife, a scissor pen, a pad and finally a water gun, then she set off.

She knew there were some woods nearby so she decided to go and explore them. When she got there she began to study the nature and trees. She didn't notice that she was wandering off the track and before she knew it, Fiona was face to face with a very old wall. She stood up and in front of her she saw a tiny cottage with an old wooden door. She opened the door and in she went!

Meanwhile at her house, her mummy and daddy were ordering servants to search for Fiona, but they had no luck. Her mother and father decided to go and look for her in the woods. They found the old cottage and went in, but just as they did that a green head with red marbles for eyes stood up. The figure was dripping with red liquid . . . it was Fiona!

Holly Fraser (8)
Little Gaddesden Primary School, Little Gaddesden, Herts

IN THE CHURCHYARD

One day in a place in Hertfordshire, there were two girls walking home from school. Those two girls were called Katie and Mildred. Katie was kind and sensitive, and Mildred was good and helpful.

'Mill, do you believe in ghosts?' Katie asked.

'Of course not!' said Mildred.

'If you don't, we shall meet in the churchyard tonight with a torch, notebook, pencil or pen, and a food supply,' said Katie.

When night came the girls sneaked out of bed and to the churchyard. When they got there, they saw something moving in the bushes. It seemed to be a silvery shadow with a black hood.

'A ghost!' said Mildred. They ducked down low behind a gate.

'You cannot hide from me!' said the ghost in an evil voice.

It came closer and closer and pulled out its huge sword. Before the ghost could stop them, they started digging his grave. The ghost disappeared into a puff of smoke.

After that night, the girls never went out at night again.

One week later, someone died at the churchyard . . .

Ella Lamport (8)
Little Gaddesden Primary School, Little Gaddesden, Herts

SPOOKS

One rainy, stormy day there lived a brother and sister, Peter and Hannah. Hannah had curly blonde hair and Peter had dark brown hair. One Friday they lost the school's brand new Frisbee when it flew into their attic.

'I'm going to find the Frisbee, otherwise we'll have to pay,' said Hannah.

'Haven't you heard about Spooks, the frightening ghost who lives in the attic? He can eat anything, he's so greedy,' said Peter.

'Well I don't care because I'm going now,' answered Hannah climbing up the ladder.

Peter was shivering as Hannah stepped in, but nothing happened. Hannah could smell dampness around her. In each corner there was a sticky cobweb. Still nothing happened to her though. Peter was amazed at this. Hannah walked forward and started looking for the Frisbee. Then she saw an open box and she thought it could have flown in it, but she was in for a surprise . . .

'Who dares enter my attic?' said a voice from behind her.

'Who's that?' asked Hannah - now scared like Peter was. She turned around and, 'Argh!'

'Hannah, are you all right?' asked Peter, but there was no answer.

The next day red liquid was dripping from the attic . . .

Sarah Hocking (8)
Little Gaddesden Primary School, Little Gaddesden, Herts

A SCARY GHOST STORY

Jessica went down the wooden, creaky stairs with her hair waving from side to side and with sleep all in her eyes. She opened the blue rusty door to let her cat Mint in. Mint rushed in and rubbed her golden fur onto Jessica's leg, like a snake climbing a tree. Jess ran up the stairs to get dressed. As she was climbing the stairs her cat ran straight up and hid in her bedroom.

'Mint, Mint, Mint, don't be a silly cat,' she said.

She walked down the old creaky stairs once again, with Mint in her arms. There was *suddenly* a tap on her head, and as soon as that happened Mint jumped straight out of Jess's arms and out of the door to the top of a tree. Jessica screamed her head off like a tiger in a mood. *Then suddenly*, there was a loud laugh, a scream and then silence.

Flora Brown (8)
Little Gaddesden Primary School, Little Gaddesden, Herts

THE GHOST DOG

Jade was ecstatic. She was going to stay in a hotel on her own while her mum was away on business. Her dad had died three years ago, so there was no one to look after her. A horn beeped outside. It was time to go. She picked up her bag, ran out of the door and jumped into the car.

When she got there, there was nothing much to do, so she went out to the hotel gardens. In the corner Jade spotted a little enclosure of bushes and she went over to check it out. In it there was only flowers to see at the front, but at the back there was the body of a dead dog. Jade stared at it in horror, then something happened which made her want to scream.

The corpse shimmered, then a misty, transparent shape of a dog formed. The ghost snarled which made Jade step back in terror. The second she moved, the dog pounced and she fell back. Her body lay there while the dog stood snarling over her, waiting for its next victim . . .

Jennifer Cannon (9)
Little Gaddesden Primary School, Little Gaddesden, Herts

THE SPOOKY FOREST

One beautiful summer's day, Tom and his friend Amy, went deep into the forest. Tom was eleven years old and his special feature was his lovely smile and he was a great footballer (nearly as good as David Beckham.) Amy was eleven as well and her special feature was a little spot under her eye and she was very clever.

Anyway, when they were walking along they both dropped and after a few seconds they found out they were sinking. Tom tried to use his football skills to get them out, but it didn't work. The sand was too strong. What could they do? Then they both remembered. *'Help!'* they shouted. But it was just a white sheet, *no a ghost!* The ghost flew as fast as he could. He got Amy, but where was the football superstar?

Tom Cullimore (8)
Little Gaddesden Primary School, Little Gaddesden, Herts

THERE IS A GHOST IN OUR PORCH

One bright, fine and sunny day there lived twins. They had a father who was always working at the police station and their mum worked in computers (she has to find out what is wrong when they crash.) The twins always wore grey dungarees and a T-shirt. They both had a different feature - Rosie had chubby cheeks and Annie had very red rosy cheeks.

That afternoon Annie and Rosie were very bored. They asked their mum what they could do. She said, 'There's some games up in the loft, if you want to try and get up there.'
Rosie replied, 'But Mum, we can't reach the ladder.'
'OK, I'll come and do it for you,' said their mum.

So their mum went upstairs and opened the loft. She got a game and passed it down to the girls. 'Do you like that game or do you want me to get you another game for you?' said Mum.
Annie replied, 'We'll stick with this one Mum?'

Suddenly there was a knock on the door. Annie went to open it. When she did there was nothing, but there was something round her neck . . . and then when her mum looked to see who it was, there going down the drive was a trail of bright red blood. Mum said, 'My darling angel is gone.'

Laura Barthorpe (9)
Little Gaddesden Primary School, Little Gaddesden, Herts

THE HAUNTED HOUSE

One day there were two people, one man and one woman. They had just moved out of their house but they couldn't find another one. The man's name was Ben and the lady's name was Amy. Amy quite often wears long silk dresses and Ben wears jeans and a dark blue T-shirt.

One day they went for a walk in the woods and they saw a house. 'Perhaps we could live there?' said Ben.
'Maybe we could,' said Amy.
'But we would have to do it up,' she said happily.

So they went to find a builder in the nearest town. They found one and his name was John. They all went back to the house and the builder said, 'You need a lot of work done but I'll get on with it.'

By Monday they were allowed to move in. They had lived there for a week when they started to hear funny noises. It sounded like a ghost, so one night Ben stayed up with a gun. He saw a very faint white shadow coming down - it was a ghost. He stayed there until the ghost had gone then he crept upstairs and told his wife.

The next day they called in the ghost killers and that night they got him and that was the end of their worries.

Adam Weaver (9)
Little Gaddesden Primary School, Little Gaddesden, Herts

A GHOST STORY

Long, long ago there were two teasable, spooky ghosts. They were called Spooky and Scary. The two ghosts lived in a dark village. All day long, the breeze sounded like an echoing sound, like a dolphin makes.

One day their mysterious house fell down and broke. One dull day the two ghosts went outside, but what did they see? A brand new perfect house. Later that day the mysterious house broke down as well.

The following day Spooky and Scary went to the old wood. In the night they found a nice old house and so they lived there forever.

Nathalie Snackaert (8)
Little Gaddesden Primary School, Little Gaddesden, Herts

THE GHOST IN THE SHED

Emma looked out of her window. The sun shone high in the sky. There wasn't a cloud in the sky. Emma's long brown hair swished around. As she walked downstairs the light made her eyes shine. Mum greeted her at the end of the stairs. 'You're up early,' she said.
'I was up all night,' replied Emma.
'Time for some breakfast I think. What about you?' said Mum.
'Okay,' said Emma.

It was the end of school and Emma set off home. When she arrived she could hear someone crying. It was coming from the shed. Emma opened the door, it creaked. There was a figure - a laughing figure. It was a man. The man looked like he was from Tudor times. In his hand was a head - a head of a woman and from her neck white was dripping. Emma gave out a loud scream and fell to the ground.

When she woke up she found herself in hospital. That night she looked in the shed and the man had gone.

Harriet Clair Whitehead (7)
Little Gaddesden Primary School, Little Gaddesden, Herts

THE HAUNTED HOTEL

One cold winter's day in the hotel there was a ghost called Hornta. Hornta decided to go and do some tricks. He knew a person called Robert. Robert wasn't scared of anything much and Hornta kept on creeping up to him. Robert didn't get tricked that easily!

Robert went for breakfast - he had the full monty. Then he went to play snooker with his dad but Hornta was following him into the games room.
'Where shall we go now?' said Robert.
'Well, you play here for a bit and I'll come down later,' said Dad.

But while Dad was upstairs, Hornta jumped out in front of Robert. Robert fainted.

An hour later Robert woke up and Dad had still not come down so Hornta said, 'I want to be friends,'
Robert said, 'Yes.'

They both went to play a few games. Then Robert's dad came down and said, 'Who's that?'
Robert said, 'It is Hornta,' and they became the best of friends.

Stephen Berry (8)
Little Gaddesden Primary School, Little Gaddesden, Herts

THE SURPRISE

In a dark, spooky wood, which no one ever went into, there lived a ghost called Oliver who was very polite to all his friends.

One day, when he went out to play, only a few of his friends came out.

One night when he was fast asleep he was woken up by a very strange noise. The noise sounded like this; 'Ha, ha, ha . . . thud!'

The thud made Oliver jump. When he got fed up with the 'Ha, ha, ha . . . thud,' he went down the stairs, out of the house and into his friend's house. But there was no one there, so he went to the edge of the wood, counted to three and then walked out of the wood, across the grass and into the other side of the wood. When he got there the noise began very loud. He was halfway through the wood when he stopped and listened. He couldn't hear the 'Ha, ha, ha . . . thud' anymore, so he went back again into the other wood. He made his first step when he heard a thud! He then saw a tape player so he turned it off and when he did so, lots ghosts appeared and they said, 'Surprise!' and they gave him a piece of cake. Everyone lived happily ever after.

Jack Elkes (8)
Little Gaddesden Primary School, Little Gaddesden, Herts

THE GHOST TRAIN

One sunny, warm summer's day there were two teenagers playing outside. They were called Sally and Neil. Sally had long blonde hair, blue eyes and was nineteen. Neil had short brown hair and brown eyes. They were both there for each other and were very good friends. Sally wore black high-heeled shoes, a long dark dress and a dark cardigan. Neil usually wore black tie-up shoes and a suit.

One afternoon they wanted to do something because they were very bored. They decided to go to the fair. At the fair they went on the big wheel.
'I hate this,' said Neil.
'Neil, I have made up a new rhyme. Neil on the wheel.'
'It's not funny,' said Neil.

Next they went on the big roller coaster. On the roller coaster Sally said, 'I think I can see a ghost.'
'Oh, don't be silly,' said a mysterious voice.
'Who said that?' said Neil.
'See, it's a ghost,' said Sally.

To see even more ghosts they went on the spooky, horrifying ghost train. They were more than halfway when Neil realised that Sally was missing. Did she get taken by the ghost? We will never ever know . . .

Kate Rogers (9)
Little Gaddesden Primary School, Little Gaddesden, Herts

WHAT HEAVEN MEANS TO ME

My image of Heaven would be:-

I arrive at enormous marble gates which would be closed. At the gates stands Jesus, the Lord God's son. Jesus would look through the thousands of pages full of names. When he found your name you would go through the marble gates, but if your name was not there you would be sent down to Hell.

I believe when you walk through the marble doors everything from then on is peaceful, kind and everyone is in good health. I believe that the grass would be green, the water would be clear and the sky would be blue. I believe that the animals would be your friends and you would be the animals' friends. You could go for long walks and feel the breeze on your face.

In Heaven no one would be angry and there would be no hatred. You could do everything that is good but nothing that is bad. I believe there is no war, no illnesses and no darkness in Heaven.

Lara Samworth (11)
Maltman's Green School, Gerrard's Cross, Bucks

A CIRCUS

It was a hot, dry Saturday. We all had nothing to do. We all decided to go to the circus - we all loved circuses.

At the circus there was a really funny, weird man. This man was riding a unicycle. The unicycle must have been really frightening to ride in front of a massive crowd. A lady in a spotted funny jacket with spotted trousers came out. Her hair was as blonde as the sun. She was now going to tight rope walk. It must be so frightening as well, and also to keep your balance so you don't fall off and be embarassed in front of a lot of strangers, must be difficult.

After, a man came out with an elephant. The elephant had huge, fat, grey ears and his body was huge and grey too. The man told us that the elephant was called Nellie.

We had to move on to a seal show. The seals were very intelligent, wet, active, slimy and able to balance on a ball on their noses. A man came out with a striped waistcoat and huge brown-laced shoes. He went to get a small blue and green spotted ball and balanced it on the slimy, wet seal's nose.

We moved a little further on to where we saw clowns. There were three clowns. One of them was wearing some spotted trousers, a striped waistcoat, big black shoes and red lipstick for red cheeks. Another of them was wearing smiley faced trousers, a flowery waistcoat, a pair of pink spotted huge slip-on shoes and purple lipstick for his spotty cheeks. The last one was wearing shells all over his trousers, rabbits all over his waistcoat, huge blue striped shoes and pink lipstick for his ugly cheeks.

After, there was a man who juggled fire for us. He then ate the burning hot fire. That was my favourite act at the fun circus. We all had a lovely, fun day. We will have to wait another boring, long six months till we can go back to the circus.

Natasha Garnham (10)
Maltman's Green School, Gerrard's Cross, Bucks

WHAT HEAVEN MEANS TO ME

If I went to Heaven I think it would be the happiest time I had ever known. Laughter, joy, truth would all be there with no sadness, hurt or injuries.

Every person's idea of paradise would be real and they would share it with other people who had the same idea of paradise as them.

I think that the different types of paradise would be separated by rivers of chocolate in which anyone could bathe.

If I saw God, I think he would be sitting on a throne of pearls and answering queries of all spirits.

My idea of Heaven's different types of paradise are images of Earth, but with no need to earn money, no pollution, hate, spite, no cities and with no people waiting on you.

People would wear simple white robes and be happy forever doing things they liked and wanted to do.

My idea of paradise is a sandy beach with palm trees shading and a chocolate hot tub. Also, there would be a clear stream leading through a cool rainforest.

In Heaven I hope to see my family and talk to them and ask them what they thought of their life on Earth.

I think that in Heaven there is no need to eat or sleep so there would be eternal light. I think that in Heaven you never grow old.

In Heaven I think that if people wanted to see their families they could go to Earth but they would only be able to make contact with one friend or relation.

If Heaven is paradise it makes life seem like just one adventure in amongst many others.

Amy Tibble (10)
Maltman's Green School, Gerrard's Cross, Bucks

TWISTS

Monday

Dear diary,
Five days till Christmas. I only have £60 out of £80. I need to buy my Game Boy. I have to earn some money quickly.
Love Amy.

Tuesday

12.00pm
Dear diary,
I have asked all round the neighbours if they want me to shovel snow off their doorsteps.
2.30pm
Mr and Mrs Slow gave me £4 for doing their door step.
Love Amy.

Wednesday

Dear diary,
I went shopping to see the prices and if they had gone down. They had not but one thing was lucky, I found a purse with £100 in it. I am going to buy my Game Boy tomorrow, I have to because Mum is going to buy me games for it as Christmas gifts.
Love Amy.

Thursday

Dear diary,
I went to the shops with my £164 because I wanted to buy some clothes with the rest of the money. I was queuing to buy the Game Boy when the man in front of me said that he had lost a purse with £100 in it. That was it! My chances of getting a Game Boy were gone. I told the man I had found his purse and gave it back. I turned to go. Then the man said, 'Wait, I didn't want the money back. Why I wanted the purse back was because it has my wife's best earrings inside. Here, have £20 as my thanks for you finding it and returning it.'

I nearly screamed for joy. I could finally get my Game Boy. I went up to the counter and paid for my Game Boy. I had finally got it. I was so happy.
Love Amy.

Friday

Dear diary,
Big disaster. Mum could not find any Game Boy games she thought I would like. She did buy me some clothes though. I am fed up. I will have to earn more money to buy Game Boy games.
Love Amy.

Eleanor Jaffa (10)
Maltman's Green School, Gerrard's Cross, Bucks

A STORY WITH A TWIST

Ruby, a rich 40-year-old, was walking in Disneyland Paris. It was a sunny dry morning and there was a queue for every good ride.

After a long time, she decided which ride she would go on. It did not have a very long queue. It was a long, boring wait until she got on the ride. However, the ride was quite amusing. Considering the time she had to wait, the ride was very short.

Ruby went on another ride. When she got off, it started to pour down with rain. She ran as fast as she could splashing through the puddles to a stand selling ponchos and decided to buy one.

When she was looking for a poncho, a handbag caught her attention. It was a brown furry bag with a Mickey Mouse on the front. It was the perfect souvenir for her, the best handbag in the world, until she saw the price tag. It was only 15 Francs. However, it was what she wanted, she could buy it and say that it cost 1,000 Francs and was real fur. Ruby bought the bag and the poncho.

As soon as she bought the poncho, it stopped raining. Ruby was not very happy and she was about to throw it away when the lady at the stand said, 'Don't throw that away! You can use that tomorrow when it rains.'
'Oh alright,' replied Ruby and walked off annoyed.

She was going to throw it away in the next bin. When she saw what it looked like she turned away disgusted by the way it looked. The bin was overflowing and flies were flying around it, ants were eating the food in the bin, but worst of all was the smell. You could smell it from two metres away so no one was going near it. Ruby decided she was going to have to keep the poncho after all, in her supposed to be real fur 1,000 Franc handbag.

Whilst she was walking, a lady stopped her and asked, 'Where did you get that beautiful handbag?'
'Oh,' said Ruby astonished, 'I bought it today in the Mickey's Expensive Goods Shop. It is one of a kind and it is real fur and leather!'
'So it is not real gold, the Mickey Mouse!'

'Of course it is!' exclaimed Ruby. 'I would not buy anything fake. As a matter of fact, it is 24 carat.'

'Be careful it does not get stolen,' whispered the lady.

'I do not think I need to take your advice!' said Ruby hautily. 'Not me!' Ruby started to walk away.

A man ran past her and before Ruby knew what was happening, he grabbed her handbag. She screamed and people started asking her, 'What is the matter?'

Ruby told them and people started running after the thief. The lady who Ruby had told about her handbag and it being one of a kind said to Ruby loudly so that everyone in the country could hear it: 'You will get your handbag back. After all, it is one of a kind, so no one will have the same as you, so people will notice it!'

'No they will not!' cried Ruby. 'It was only 15 Francs. I made everything up!' She started to cry.

The crowd started to whisper. Then someone shouted, 'She made it up about the handbag!'

Somehow, the thief must have heard this, because he stopped where he was. A security man came up to him, put handcuffs on him and said, 'You are arrested for robbing this lady of her handbag.'

Jacqueline Rumens (11)
Maltman's Green School, Gerrard's Cross, Bucks

BLACK BEAUTY - NEW CHAPTER 2

I was sad to leave my mother. I knew it was for the best but I really wanted to stay. My mother reminded me to always do my best and always keep up my good name.

Old Daniel put on my halter and tied me to the back of his cart. The chickens clucked noisily in the back of the cart and the cart horses whinnied their goodbyes, then we set off.

The market was seven miles away; we met many farmers on the way. They had a large variety of livestock, starting from piglets, chickens and lambs, ending at fully-grown shire horses.

When we reached the market all the horses were put in stalls, almost immediately we were looked at by men. They looked at our feet and our teeth, they made sure we were in good health.

At the auction old Daniel lead me into the ring. The auctioneer said, 'Fine thoroughbred - grandfather won the cup in two Newmarket races. Bid starting at £15.'
Bids rattled back like hailstones
'£16!' '£17!' '£18!' '£19!' '£20!' '£21!' . . . '£26!'
Then the auctioneer bellowed, 'Going once, going twice. Sold to the man in the green cloak!'

The man took me home and put me in a large stable. Hay and straw plastered the cobbled floor and there were two empty holders where the water and food buckets should be. There was also a hay net, filled to almost bursting.

A while later a small girl came into the stable and stroked me. She was soft and gentle. So different from the man, who was rough and uncaring. She gave me food and some water, then she tacked me up ready for use. I wondered if she was going to ride me and if she was a good rider.

A good while later she came and fetched me from my stable. A rich-looking man stood watching us. I guessed he was the owner of this large estate. Emily, as the girl was called, climbed onto my back and rode me to the front of the manor house. It was massive.

From one of the lower grand windows a wealthy-looking woman, obviously the mistress, watched us, staring critically at my every move.

Emily was good and kind but the rest of the estate was cold and hard. I wondered what was in store for me here. Was I going to like it?

Jessica Try (11)
Maltman's Green School, Gerrard's Cross, Bucks

SMITH LEARNS TO READ

Smith walked huffily down the stone, cold steps. Upon realising that he hadn't eaten since dinner the night before, Smith searched the street with his eyes for something to eat, while keeping on the lookout for someone to teach him how to read.

He spotted a large house about eighty yards along the road. Smith was starving and so he decided he would sprint to the house. Before he reached the large manor house, he slowed down because he had a sharp pain in the side of his chest. So he half-walked, half-jogged the rest of the distance.

When Smith reached the garden fence he put one leg over the fence but as he put his weight onto the other side he tripped over. As he picked himself back up, he could smell freshly baked bread and realised that the smell was coming from an open door around the side of the house. Smith tiptoed round to the side of the house and peered in. He couldn't see anyone inside so he crept in and looked around the room that he was standing in.

It was larger than the room which he and his sisters owned, which was situated below an inn. This room smelled strongly of many different kinds of food, such as apple pie and blackcurrant crumble. The strongest smell of all though, was the warm bread, whose smell wafted through the open door. Smith stretched out his hands to tear off a piece of crispy bread. Before his fingers touched the bread he heard a screech. 'Stop! Stop! You thieving little scoundrel. What do you think you're doing?'
'I'm sorry ma'am. I'm just so very hungry.'
'I don't care,' she replied. 'I won't have you stealing the food that I've worked so hard to make tasty for the master.'

Smith was a tough boy but this was just too much for him and he just broke down and started to sob. The cook looked down at this poor boy, who was wearing rags. Even though she had been so horrible to him, she felt pity in the depths of her heart.

'No one will teach me to read,' sobbed Smith.

'I will darling,' she replied. 'I will.'

Michelle Louisa Cathcart (11)
Maltman's Green School, Gerrard's Cross, Bucks

BAD LUCK!

Mandy, Molly and May Goodman were triplets, sharing their birthday on the 7th June. In their large family there were five children: Mandy, Molly, May, Peter and Richard. The triplets were identical, with golden hair and hazel eyes. Peter was small with dark hair and extremely dark eyes. He was seven. Richard was the same as Peter, with dark hair and very dark eyes. He was fourteen.

With such a large family they struggled to buy things. This year the triplets were trying to buy each other something special for the ninth birthdays.

Mandy sat in the corner of their sunset bedroom chewing the end of her pencil and looking down at her clipboard, where she had attached some paper.

Molly had gone out of the room, supposedly to ask their mother for ideas. Meanwhile, May lay over her tartan rug thoughtfully looking around the room and on the bookshelves for ideas. They were all thinking of what to buy each other for their birthdays. All the girls had the same thing in their mind: they needed money to by each other presents.

Molly and Mrs Goodman suddenly appeared in the doorway. Mrs Goodman then blurted out, 'I know you need money to buy each other presents but at the moment we have hardly any money. Five pounds was all that I could save. But don't worry!'
Turning to leave, she stopped to think.
'What are you doing Mother?' chorused the children.
'I've got a super idea!' she then paused, you could find something you don't really need and swap it with one of your friends at school for a present you know the other two would like!'
'Okay,' replied the triplets.
There was a mad dash around the room as they all tried to find something that they could swap with other girls at school.

After hours of searching they found the items. Mandy found her old watch which had tattered edges but, using the scissors, she cut most of these off. Then she went to phone her friend Rosie, to see if she had anything nice. Explaining the whole situation, Rosie then immediately offered her a shiny platinum keyring. Mandy was thrilled. She decided to give it to Molly for she was longing for a nice keyring to put on her cheap leopard-skin handbag.

Meanwhile, Molly had found her leopard-skin handbag and said, 'You are the only respectable item that I own worth swapping with someone.' She went off sulking but it had to be done. She went to phone her friend, Claire. Claire already knew the family were poor because she had been to their house so often.
She answered, 'I could give you some dolls' clothes for May because I know she likes dolls!'
'Oh thank you! She will simply love them. Can you bring them into school tomorrow?'
'Oh yes,' replied Claire.
'By the way, you can have my leopard-skin handbag,' said Molly.
'Thanks,' replied Claire, who then hung up.
Molly ran off, skipping happily.
May then found her doll and said to it, 'You will have to be swapped for something else at school.'

The next morning May went to Georgina, who offered her a metal watchstrap for Mandy. May thought this was so perfect she immediately did the swap.

When they got home they all wrapped their presents in different rooms. Mandy stayed in their bedroom and wrapped Molly's present in a shiny blue paper. Molly went into the kitchen and wrapped May's present in a gold paper, then in black writing she wrote 'Happy Birthday!' May sat in the lounge wrapping Mandy's present in a red and silver paper. They all wrote their cards at bedtime. They then stuck them on their presents and hid them again, ready for the next day.

In the morning the girls raced downstairs. The parents were already there with Peter and Richard. Mandy grabbed her gift first. She ripped off the paper and found the metal watchstrap. Her stomach lurched. She put on a false smile for the rest of the family.

'Well Mandy, do you like it? asked Mrs Goodman.

'Yes I do, thank you May,' said Mandy staring at the strap the whole time.

'Can I open mine now?' said Molly obviously filled with excitement.

'Yes dear,' said Mr Goodman.

She eagerly tore off the paper and saw the platinum keyring. She opened her mouth to speak but decided not to. Then she said in a small voice. 'It's nice!'

'My turn!' shouted May. She lunged for her present and pulled it open. Inside were several Barbie outfits and several pairs of Barbie shoes. She was so shocked. She didn't say anything though. 'They're lovely,' said May eventually. Then there was silence.

Mandy suddenly blurted out, 'I sold my watch to buy Molly this keyring for her bag!'

'I sold my bag to buy May some dolls' clothes!' said Molly.

'I then sold my doll to buy the watchstrap for Mandy!' added May.

Their parents looked shocked whilst the triplets looked at each other.

'Oh well dears!' said Mrs Goodman, laughing a bit, 'you've had a bit of bad luck. But remember, it's the thought that counts!'

Slowly they realised what had happened, but luckily they saw the funny side of it.

Claire McIlvenny (10)
Maltman's Green School, Gerrard's Cross, Bucks

THE LADY OF SHALOT

When I was younger my mother told me that a witch had put a curse upon me. Her conclusion was that should I look at Camelot, the curse would be activated. We lived in a castle near Camelot on the island of Shalot. The window does not face Camelot, but you can see it if you look out of the window. When I was ten years of age I went up into the tower. We hung a mirror high on the wall where I could look and see the reflection of the road to Camelot, but not see Camelot itself. I have lived this way for seven years.

I was sitting weaving at my loom when a man on horseback passed. He wasn't any old man. He had beautiful coal black curls hanging on his shoulders from under his silver helmet. His eyes were sparkling, his armour so bright it was dazzling. A jewel encrusted sword hung from his saddle, his horse was sleek and black with a jewel encrusted bridle. I had seen the man of my dreams. His name was Sir Lancelot, one of the knights of the Round Table of King Arthur.

Without thinking, I rushed to the window. I saw him clearly now. I saw the fields and I saw Camelot. The curse was upon me. Behind me, the mirror cracked, everything shattered. I put on a white wedding dress that I had stored in my chest. I ran to the bottom of the tower and out of the door. I wrote 'Lady of Shalot' around the prow of the boat, turning the boat face towards Camelot. I climbed into the boat and pushed it off the side of the river bank. I was becoming weaker and weaker. I was finding it more and more difficult to breathe. I knew then that I would be dead soon and never see Lancelot or Camelot again.

The boat drifted into Camelot safely. Word spread that I was in the castle and everyone came to the bank to look at me. King Arthur and his queen, Guinevere, with many others that came to see, Sir Lancelot was among them.

'Why has this beautiful woman died?' he asked aloud. Little did he know that he was the reason, he was the one who had cost me my life.

Charlotte Greene (10)
Maltman's Green School, Gerrard's Cross, Bucks

ONE RING

I lay in my bed alone. My head was swimming with thoughts of the ring. I heard a rustling in the trees. Was it the ring bearers coming to find and kill me? I felt around for the ring. I found the pouch and tipped it out. I looked at the ring, it had some form of writing around the middle. It looked elfish. Gandalf had told me it said, 'One ring to rule them all'. How could one ring cause such trouble?

My bed felt hard. I tossed and turned and then, I just lay rigid in my bed for the last time. I heard footsteps coming up the staircase. It was Bilbo. He walked into my bedroom and sat on my bed.
'Bilbo?'
'Yes Frodo.'
'I'm frightened.'
'Yes I know, so I am.'
'Bilbo?'
'Yes Frodo.'
'Why did you give the ring to Gandalf?'
'My dear Frodo, I was becoming evil, the ring was taking over me, my life.'
'Why didn't Gandalf take the ring to Mount Doom?'
'Gandalf has such power, he would be tempted to use the ring.'
'Frodo, may I . . .'
'No Bilbo.'
'Please.'
'Bilbo, I can't let you.'
'Oh . . . Frodo, I wouldn't do anything.'
'Bilbo.'
'Goodnight Frodo.'
'Goodbye Bilbo.'
'No, until we meet again.'
'Yes, until we meet again,' and he was gone.

I lay on my bed. I was never going to sleep tonight. I climbed out of bed and walked over to the window. I felt frightened, yet another part of me felt privileged to have been given such an honour. I knew the other ring bearers were after Bilbo so he would have to leave too. I was glad that I would have Sam for company. I wished that I could be brave and strong on the inside and outside. How could a small hobbit like I be expected to carry such power and succeed? I wished that I could be a great wizard, like Gandalf. I could tell he was tempted but I was the chosen one, why? I am neither strong nor wise but I am not foolish. I am neither brave nor timid. I have none of Gandalf's qualities. Why is he a wizard and I am not?

My last thought before going to sleep was, why me?

Charlotte Mort (11)
Maltman's Green School, Gerrard's Cross, Bucks

THE SEINE AT ARGENTEUIL

I, Lady Victoria, was sitting outside my house. It was a very sunny afternoon and as usual I had taken my son Patrick and my daughter Jane down to paddle by the river. My husband, Lord Andrew, always refused to come and today he said to me, 'One day you'll regret it.'

I was surprised and I sat outside thinking about what he had just said until I was interrupted by the children.

We all live in Paris with the river Seine running half a mile away from our house. My daughter is four and my son is six. I love them very much. I do not think I could bear living without them. We are very rich but we try to act like a normal family.

It was July and the temperature was above thirty degrees Celsius. I put the children to bed and read them a story. When I tucked them in I thought, I hope things never change.

The next day though I found that things did change. Again it was a very hot day and I planned to take the children down to the river. It was about one o'clock in the afternoon when we went. We arrived about ten minutes later. I sat down on the soft grass and watched my children paddling in the river. Then I heard it - a scream, 'Mummy, Mummy!'

I opened my eyes; I must have been asleep. I looked over to the river and there was little Jane being swept down the river, bobbing up and down on the surface. Then a thought went into my head, she could not swim.
'Jane!' I screamed, 'Kick your legs.'
I could not swim either so I did not have a chance of rescuing her.
'Patrick, get Daddy!' I shouted to him.

Andrew and Patrick came running back five minutes later to find me weeping by the side of the river. There was no hope of rescuing her now.
'Where is she?' asked my husband.
I weakly answered back, 'She's gone.'

Nothing was the same without Jane. A week later Patrick and I went down to the river. We stood there and then I remembered my husband's words, 'One day you'll regret it.' I thought how happy we had been the week before. I thought of the river and how I had loved it so much, but now I hated it. Lastly, I thought of little Jane. I stood with Patrick and thought of nothing but little Jane.

Hannah Johnston (10)
Maltman's Green School, Gerrard's Cross, Bucks

FRODO'S FEELINGS

I have been asked to take this ring and destroy it. I feel honoured because I have been asked to do this; I am however, very frightened because I may die. Gandalf has told me that if the ring gets into the wrong hands we might die, so we have to be careful.

Sam has overheard what Gandalf has told me, so Sam also must come along with us. If I put the ring on then I will become invisible, which is sort of exciting. It's not often a boy my age gets to go on such an exciting trip.

I suppose I am taking this the wrong way. I am not meant to get over-excited you know, this is serious. I have no idea why my uncle has gone, and why he has left his ring in my possession. I don't know why he has left me to do this on my own. Well, at least I have Gandalf and my best friend Sam. I am sure Gandalf has thought about this and knows how to get there and the safest route to take there. I am just worried because if people try to kill me while I'm asleep and take the ring, then it will fall into the wrong hands, so the whole world could die. This is a difficult task.

Clare Davis (11)
Maltman's Green School, Gerrard's Cross, Bucks

A DAY IN THE LIFE OF TOM THE CHIMNEY SWEEP

A boy named Tom, an apprentice to a chimney sweep, lived in 1837. He lived a hard life, though he thought his life was normal. The master he had was cruel to him and the other four boys he cleaned with, one of which he liked.

Tom woke one morning, a layer of mist covered some of the chimneys, which he knew he had swept or would sweep soon. He set off to find his master. Tom found him along with the other boys, leaning against a wall. When Tom greeted his master, he got a sharp stare as if his master was saying, I'll beat you if you're late again. Tom's master gave him a slice of bread and they all set off.

They reached the house that they were cleaning that day. After they had been let into the house they started cleaning. Soot covered their faces, their clothes went black, their joints got scraped and they got beaten. Two hours later Tom's master collected his money and they left.

Their master left them to find their own way back. They all split up. Tom ran back to where he had slept the previous night to play with his friends. He played throw and catch with half pennies, leapfrog over posts and bowling stones at the horses.

Tom found a small piece of bread, which somebody had dropped. He ate it quickly as he had an early start again in the morning.

Michelle Katz (11)
Maltman's Green School, Gerrard's Cross, Bucks

THE TWIST

One pound and ten pence was all Sophie had. It was Christmas Day tomorrow and Sophie had to get something for her best friend Sabrina. Sabrina had a flute and would hate to be parted from it.

Sabrina was at her home counting all her money. One pound and nine pence was all she had. She would never be able to buy Sophie a present and then remembered her necklace. It was a silver heart and when you opened it, there was a picture of her mother and father because she was an orphan.

She went into the market and saw a jewellery shop. Sabrina then said, 'Oh my, that chain for her necklace looks lovely, especially when her old chain had a knot in it.' She went into the shop and realised that she couldn't afford it, so she asked the lady, 'Do you like this flute? I need to exchange something for that chain over there.'
'I guess so,' the shopkeeper sighed. So Sabrina gave the flute to the shopkeeper and the shopkeeper gave the chain to Sabrina in a special case.

Back at Sophie's house, Sophie was thinking of what she should get Sabrina. She decided to go and take a trip to the market place. While she was wandering around she saw this shop called 'Famous Musicians'. It had lovely instruments. She went in there and one of the people said, 'Isn't that a lovely necklace you're wearing, young lady?'
'Yes, thank you. Do you have any flute cases?'
'Why, of course we do,' he answered. She couldn't afford it and asked him if she could swap the necklace for the flute and it was done!

It was Christmas Day and Sabrina and Sophie couldn't wait to give each other their presents. So after they had their dinner, they sat down and ripped their presents open. They were both so surprised. Then Sophie started saying, 'I swapped my flute for your flute case.'
Sabrina replied, 'I swapped my flute for your chain, but I guess we did something right; besides Christmas is all about caring and loving and that is just what we did!'

Carlotta Eden (11)
Maltman's Green School, Gerrard's Cross, Bucks

TWISTER

Mark gave a deep sigh as he gazed out of the window. Sophia was there. Beautiful Sophia. There she was, walking along jauntily, bouncing her curly golden hair on her shoulders. He stood up slowly and began pacing the room. He wanted to get her a gift. A present which would make her bright blue eyes sparkle with delight. But what? He glanced at his watch. Half an hour until the shops closed. Quickly he pulled on his coat and strode out of the door to the shops.

He stared at the shop window. He had known Sophia for three years. He remembered the way in which she spoke, with a laughing, childish air, the way she danced light as a feather and twice as graceful as any swan. He couldn't get her chocolates - she had lovely ones of her own. She had a great collection of jewellery, from moonstone earrings to the finest pearl necklace, and flowers just weren't special enough.

Suddenly a movement caught his eye. In another shop window a man was putting up a sign that read, *Dresses half-price*. Mark walked doubtfully towards the window. Dresses weren't exciting enough somehow. However, he was wrong. A brilliant, sparkling blue dress with lacy bows and an elegant collar with satin lining hung on a stand. It was perfect, he could just see Sophia at the ball the following evening glimmering in the dress, saying in that musical voice of hers, 'Marcus Stone, will you marry me?'

Yes, he decided, I'll give her this dress to wear at the ball and then, in front of everyone there, I'll propose marriage!

In the next street another man, Frank, also sat brooding over what to buy Sophia. 'A dress to wear to the ball would be useful and pretty,' he thought aloud. 'Yes, a dress to shine out amongst all the other dresses.'

He leapt up suddenly. There was not a dress shop, but a shop selling bits 'n' bobs. Frank cautiously stepped inside. On a rail was the most divine dress he had ever seen. It was a golden dress, with white hearts embroidered across the middle and silver puffs on the sleeves. He bought it and hurried home.

The next day, Sophia was surprised by two men suddenly bursting in on her quiet home.

'Sophia, I . . .'

'Look what I got . . .'

Their voices trailed off into silence as they saw Sophia. Slowly she stood up. 'You brought me presents?' she inquired in a sugary voice. Dumbstruck by her beauty, both men nodded. 'Can I see them?' she asked, tossing her long hair over her shoulder and batting her eyelashes. Both men handed over their gifts.

'Dresses?' she said disdainfully, dropping the sweet tone at once. She sighed, and tossed the dresses onto a chair where they lay crumpled in a heap. 'You may go now,' she said haughtily.

Frank was astounded. He opened his mouth to speak but Sophia swept past him opening the door to go outside.

'But what are you going to wear tonight, at the ball?' Mark called after her. She stopped suddenly and turned around. 'Oh, you'll see,' she said with a nasty laugh. 'You'll see.'

At the ball were women in colourful gowns, men with dark suits, tables covered with white linens, food and drink to satisfy a whole army, but the men looked only for one person - Sophia. Weaving their way in and out of the dancing couples, they craned their necks for a glimpse of their Sophia. They had no luck in finding her.

Suddenly a commotion started at the front, then all went silent. In stepped Sophia in robes of pure white, with a white lily tucked into her hair, and a string of pearls around her neck. She was not alone. Clasping her hand was a man. He was very handsome with a black moustache and well-brushed hair. 'This is my fiancé,' she said with a smile. 'He proposed this morning. Do you like this dress he brought me?'

Jennifer Harper (11)
Maltman's Green School, Gerrard's Cross, Bucks

A Day In The Life Of Tom

At the crack of dawn every morning Tom had to get up and go downstairs. He was allowed just a little bit of breakfast and a glass of water. After that they would set off, on foot or in a horse and carriage, to houses all over England to clean other people's chimneys. Three boys or more would go to the same house if it had more than fifteen chimneys. Tom or one of the other children, had to climb up a chimney and every time they climbed up the chimney their knees would go red raw and bleed, and the skin would start to peel off because their legs were the only things supporting them. If they got stuck up the chimney, their master or the housekeeper lit the fire underneath them so that they had to travel up towards the top of the chimney because it got so hot.

When Tom finished his job he was sent back to the workhouse. They would all play together in the garden, playing leapfrog and tossing half pennies. When dinner was served they were only allowed a bit of dinner, just some bread and something small, then they were sent to bed.

Lily Cove (11)
Maltman's Green School, Gerrard's Cross, Bucks

THE SEINE AT ARGENTEUIL

On a sunny day in Argenteuil, Marie and Lucy were waiting for a ship. They were going to Spain to visit Lucy's father.

When Lucy was born, her mother died. Lucy's father went to live in Spain, but Lucy stayed in France with her aunt Marie.

After a long wait it was finally time for Marie and Lucy to board the ship. They had paid to have a second class cabin but luckily the steward allowed them to stay in a first class room as there were not many people on-board. Lucy and Marie ran out on deck as the ship left Argenteuil.

On the fourth day there was a raging storm with cold winds and rain. After the storm a beautiful rainbow formed.

That evening the ship arrived in Spain. Lucy's father was waiting for them. They all went to see a flamenco dance and afterwards went for a delicious supper. During supper Lucy's father told them that he was going to get married to a lady called Christine and he wanted both Lucy and Marie to be bridesmaids. A few days later came the marriage.

After the wedding Lucy and Marie lived with Christine and Lucy's father in Spain where everyone was happy.

Vanessa Lea (10)
Maltman's Green School, Gerrard's Cross, Bucks

ONE RING TO RULE THEM ALL

'This is the ring that will rule them all,' whispered Gandalf, as he put his hand in his crimson cloak. He pulled out a plum coloured cloth. Carefully he opened it . . . inside was a golden ring that flashed in the dazzling light.

Suddenly, Gandalf stood up. He walked to the fireplace. Carefully he placed the ring into the heart of the fire. As it started to glow, Gandalf took the poker laying beside the fire, and scooped it out. 'Look!' hissed Gandalf. He held out the ring in his hand. There was elfish writing carved into the majestic ring. I had never seen such beauty in my life.
'You will be the one who will demolish this ring. You are to journey to Mount Doom, where you are to throw it into the raging fire,' Gandalf carried on.
Confused I asked, 'Why me? And why does this magnificent ring need to be annihilated?'
'Why?' Gandalf roared, 'This ring is villainous! The soul who has this ring, may not be evil or selfish, but whoever tries it on too much will become overwhelmed. You must take it, as you are the only hobbit that is trusted by many people. The world lies in your hands, or else it will turn to evil. Good luck, young Frodo. Remember, never put the ring on, as it will draw the evil closer.'

Gandalf took the plum covered cloth from the chipped table and placed the miraculous ring inside. Meticulously, he placed it in my trembling hand and then rushed to the front door. He pulled open the door, walked through and closed the door carelessly.

I ran to the wooden door and bolted it. I was terrified. Questions ran through my bursting head. What do the evil look like? Will there be people to help me? Why do I have to do this? What about Bilbo?

I ran to my comforting bed and climbed in. I tucked myself under the warm blankets, while clenching the frightening golden ring. All night I thought about the terrifying adventures I might have, but also about what could happen to me. I didn't want to go, but I had to. I was unable to sleep that night, so I packed and got ready for my frightening adventure yet . . .

Katarina Tencor (11)
Maltman's Green School, Gerrard's Cross, Bucks

SKELLIG

As I walked into the room, I was shivering. I was so scared. I don't know why, I just was.

Mina and I were standing watching Skellig eating his food that the owls had brought him.

Skellig called for us to go nearer to him. I couldn't move. Mina held my hand and pulled me with her towards Skellig. He told us to hold hands and walk round.

There was power. I don't know where it came from, but we were generating power. It came from all of us as a group.

Suddenly, I felt my shoulder blades ache, it was like something was trying to push through. Opening my eyes I looked at Mina and Skellig, then I looked behind me. Amazed, not believing what was happening to me, I looked down to find myself levitating above the floor and spinning around and around. All three of us were flying and we had wings rising from our shoulder blades, like we were angels. I was scared.

I closed my eyes again, trying to make myself believe that it was all a dream, though when I opened my eyes, this time Mina and Skellig had their eyes opened too. I wanted to let go, I felt I had to let go, though Mina and Skellig told me not to, so J closed my eyes trying to think of something else.

Mina squeezed my hand tighter and tighter. It felt as if she was more scared than I was. I opened my eyes again, Mina's were too. Her face was white, though when she turned her head it went silver. I thought I was too but Mina reassured me that I wasn't.

Skellig then opened his eyes and gave a grunt, he then let go of my hand so I let go of Mina's, we then slowly drifted to the ground and our wings, as if my magic, went away. Soon I found myself in a heap on the ground with Mina helping me up.

Skellig then told us both to go home so we both ran downstairs and when we were outside I asked Mina whether it was all for real. She didn't answer.

Rosanna Ward (11)
Maltman's Green School, Gerrard's Cross, Bucks

THE LADY OF SHALOT

There is a curse upon me as I sit here weaving all day. Sometimes I wish I was dead but I am too young to die. I am so lonely. I can remember being told by my parents that I was different and they too left me. Why do I have this curse?

Lancelot, Sir Lancelot, he is coming. I can hear the jingle of the bells on his bridle. I've missed seeing him reflected in my mirror. I was fifteen when I last saw him. Here he comes. How handsome he is with his fire red feathers in his helmet and his beautiful horse - diamonds and gems glitter on the saddle and bridle as he rides through Camelot. How brave he looks, glistening like a star as the sun shines on his armour. His curly black hair so soft and shiny. I must go and see him, but I will see Camelot. Hold on, it may be a lie. Perhaps I have simply been locked up in a tower. It is a lie, a complete lie? I'll go and see him, I feel the fresh air on my face. There he is. How handsome he really is.

The awful sound of a mirror cracking resounds around me. The mirror, it has cracked from side to side. The curse has come upon me. Why did I look at him, why? I must prepare. I shall wear my wedding dress and go in my boat tonight to Camelot. I will carve my name around the bow, float down the river and die. My body will float into Camelot and whoever finds me, shall bury me. Let me die softly.

Francesca Harris (10)
Maltman's Green School, Gerrard's Cross, Bucks

What Heaven Means To Me

When I think of Heaven I imagine this: My soul floats up into the clouds and there is a brilliant light, each cloud is a creamy yellow. I step forwards to see the pearly gates and I open them to see Jesus sitting on a chair with a long list. He ticks off your name and tells you if any of your relatives are there waiting to see you. When you step forwards you see a mighty temple.

There is a sign saying *Beach, Countryside, Transporter and Rooms.* If you walk towards the *Rooms* sign and follow it, it brings you to a white building. When you go inside, there is a counter with an angel sitting behind it. She gives you a multicoloured key and then you hold your key to a scanner and you are magically transported to your room.

Your room is exactly the room you always wished for. Mine would have a huge, soft bed with lots of pillows and a purple bedspread. Purple flowers would be everywhere and the room has a really soft carpet. At your bedside there are a series of buttons which can transport you to anywhere in the building. There is a self-service restaurant and you can eat as much as you like. No rubbish or dirt anywhere, no dark alleys. Everyone is kind, happy and healthy. There is a school and you can choose which days to go, but you have to go at least three times a week. School starts at nine o'clock and finishes at three o'clock.

The transporter takes you back to Earth. You get on-board, say your destination, arrive but cannot be seen by anybody.

On the days when you are not at school, you can do anything you like; ski, play on the beach or go out to lunch. Everything is free, there is no poverty. You pay with love, care and favours. No one is better than anyone else and everyone is equal.

Georgia Cosslett (10)
Maltman's Green School, Gerrard's Cross, Bucks

OH HENRY ENDING

I had previously entered the Christmas lottery knowing that there would be a very slim chance of me winning. I had tried to save all the spare money we had. Three years and I still might not win!

Paul said it was a waste of money and we were being foolish hoping. The reason I wanted the money was because this year I wanted Christmas to be special. I wanted there to be laughter and happiness instead of dullness and sadness.

It's so hard on Paul trying to get a job. No one will take him on because of how he looks. His clothes are torn and ragged. He has hollow cheeks and dark circles under his eyes. If only everyone knew just how clever he is, with maths and science especially - he's training to be an accountant.

A week before Christmas and we hadn't had a call back or anything to do with the Christmas lottery. We switched on the little black and white television in the corner of the room and clung to each other.

This was it; we weren't going to win. I just knew it. Now our hopes were a million to one. Paul was going to turn it off but I pleaded with him not to. I couldn't believe it, it had our first number - 7 yes, 2 yes, 21 yes, 5 yes and 32 yes, yes, yes!

We jumped for joy, laughing, singing, crying and dancing. I was sure this Christmas would be special. We could buy extra clothes and have a couple of potatoes and maybe even a turkey.

Paul however was sitting quietly in a corner muttering to himself. My first thought was, oh no, what if he thinks it's all been a mix up. When I slowly edged towards him he leapt up and embraced me tightly. I said I would go and collect the money.

The next day I set off wearing my best Sunday clothes; a tatty dress and plain shoes. What greeted me was enough to make anyone feel weak at the knees.

Swarms of people yelling and shouting, people in white coats and reporters writing frantically everything a little harassed man was saying.

I thought, great, a step to fame, and answered all the questions the news reporter asked me. The small man reappeared and ushered me into his office. He spoke to me quickly and quietly. It made me realise there was a problem. The money had disappeared. It must have been stolen. I couldn't believe it. All that excitement for nothing.

My mind flashed back to the newspaper reporter's question, 'How do you feel about all this trauma?' he had asked. I laughed coldly remembering that I'd said it was the most exciting day of my life and wondered how stupid that would look in the newspaper.

I trudged home tired, deflated and unhappy. How terrible. What on earth would Paul think? I opened the door and gasped. In the centre of the table stood a bulky parcel wrapped in cheap paper and red string. Paul sat grinning with triumph and he whispered gently, 'I've got it, I've got the job!'

At that point I burst into tears and told him everything I knew. By the end of it his smile still did not falter. He said, 'Don't you see, I've got a job with over £1500 pay a week, a job, I tell you a job!'

At this point I smiled and realised Christmas this year would be a special one.

Lucy Gillam (11)
Maltman's Green School, Gerrard's Cross, Bucks

BLACK BEAUTY - THE NEW CHAPTER 2

I can remember running in the field, my mother grazing whilst the farmer was ploughing the field with May, another horse. Suddenly, Ben the stable boy, came up and spoke softly to me whilst putting a head-collar on, walked me to the gate and shouted, 'Got him Sir!'

Master released May into the field and came over to the trap where Blay was tied. He tied me up at the back of the trap and got in. Once up, he walked Blay on and I trotted behind. I called to Blay. 'Where am I going?'
'You're going to the market at Green Town,' he called back, 'you're going to be sold!'

A wave of worry came over me. I remembered what my mother said. 'The people are horrible, they pinch your legs, prod your teeth and fiddle with you! I hope you are never sold, my sweet.'

We were coming up to a large open-air building with people around the outside of it. Master untied me and led me into the ring. No one else was in there but me. Master led me around in walk, then trot, then canter. Ben put a nosebag on me. Meanwhile people said, 'One guinea,' then up to twenty guineas.

The man counting stopped. The same man shouted, 'Going, going, gone!'

An old man walked over, lifted my tail and felt down my legs. It was horrid. This man took me to his cart and tied me up. A young horse said to me, 'Who are you and where do you come from?'
I replied, 'I am Black Beauty and I come from a . . . field! Who are you?'
'I am Merry-legs and I come from a . . . farm, you are coming to live with Ginger and I,' said the cart horse huffily.

The man got into the trap and we set off.

Verity Groom (10)
Maltman's Green School, Gerrard's Cross, Bucks

SMITH LEARNS TO READ

Smith turned and trudged out of the heavy wooden church door fuming, disappointed, feeling frustrated. He turned and started to head home. After a while he became tired and sat down on a bench by the roadside. Soon a black carriage pulled up alongside attached to two elegant white horses. A man stepped out in a black suit.

'Thank you my man,' he said gratefully to the driver, as the carriage trundled away down the road he turned and saw Smith sitting alone, sobbing on the bench.
'What's wrong boy?' asked the man curiously.
Smith, seeing this as an opportunity to learn to read, lied. 'Oh sir,' said Smith. 'My two sisters have fallen ill and I fear that if they do not get help soon, they will die.'
'Don't worry,' replied the man, 'I'm a doctor and I can help them.'
'Oh, but I don't have any money to pay you. If you learned me to read you could give me recipe for a cure. Oh learn me to read Sir, learn me to read!'
'Well, when I am not working I suppose I could teach you,' replied the doctor, 'after all, it is my job to cure people.'
'Thank you, oh thank you,' cried Smith. 'When can we start?'
'Well, you meet me at my surgery tomorrow afternoon, it is the red brick building down by the baker's at Walkers Street.'
'Right!' replied Smith. 'Bye then.'

The doctor turned and strode off. Smith rubbed his hands together and smiled wickedly to himself. He had done it. Soon he would be rich.

Emma-Tina Segall (11)
Maltman's Green School, Gerrard's Cross, Bucks

INVENTIONS

Inventions. What would we do without them? Like the pen, I don't know who invented it but it was a very good idea. We use them to write things down. If we didn't write things down how would we learn things? We need to write letters to people and we need to record things in books and on paper. Scientists record things all the time. They record things about our body so that we can get to know how we work. If we didn't have pens we would have to use chalk or slate. We might even have to carve things out of stone. If we didn't write we wouldn't learn what letters and words mean so we probably wouldn't be able to read. We use pens at school and adults use them at work. We use them to write stories, poems and factual things every single day. At school they are used for exams and tests. I think that whoever invented pens wanted to invent them because he or she was tired of writing with pencils or slates.

However, while we are at school using pens we forget that we have to get to school, mostly in a car or on a bike. Who came up with the idea of inventing a car? People rely on cars. If we didn't have cars we wouldn't be able to get very far at all. Some people wouldn't be able to get to school or work. Most people work in London and they live over ten miles away. If we didn't have cars we would have to use a horse and cart like in the olden days. That wouldn't be so bad. However, horses are quite slow, so it would take rather a long time to get anywhere.

While we are having all of the luxuries that we are having, the people of America are now living in fear because of what happened to the Twin Towers and the Pentagon. It wasn't just the planes crashing that made the towers crumble, it was also the bombs that were inside the planes. Bombs are terrible things that are used when countries or people are fighting. If we didn't have them, the world wouldn't be war-free, but it would be a lot safer and more peaceful. I don't know who invented them, but I am sure it wasn't a very pleasant person. I think that it was a man who invented them (because it is usually man who is behind all the wars and fights) and probably wanted to invent them because he wanted to show everyone, that here was a man who would win a war with just a few soldiers and his bombs.

Basically, he was a man who wanted to show off his spitefulness through terrorism. If I went back in time I would stop the man and talk to him about what bombs would do to the world and how they would make the world an unsafe place.

Rebecca Pianta (10)
Maltman's Green School, Gerrard's Cross, Bucks

SOMETHING NICE

Knock! Knock! 'Coming,' I called as I slowly walked towards our tattered old front door, which we had since we moved in together twenty years ago.

As I slowly, but worriedly, approached the door, it went through my head who it could possibly be. I'm not expecting a package, Ian and I haven't ordered anything, it's far too late for the milkman as the sun is about to set and it can't be Ian because he has his own keys.

Knock! Knock! 'All right, I'm coming, hold your horses.' The gentle knock had now turned into a steady thump on the door.
'Sorry Julie, I've forgotten my keys at work,' Ian said severely as he stomped past me and down the hall after I had opened the door.
'What is wrong dear, you seem very worried?' I shouted as I walked down the hall with my voice echoing through our dingy flat. We had very little furniture, therefore whatever we said would echo through the house.

I slowly walked into the living room to find my husband spreading his long slim body over the sofa watching television. 'What is wrong dear?' I repeatedly quietly.
'Nothing, apart from the fact we don't have much money, we don't have a proper house, only a rented one, and my boss is coming over for dinner in two days and I'd like to make a good impression because he might give me a promotion. So that would mean I have to have my own house, I would have to have beautiful furniture, but lucky for you dear, I wouldn't need a lovely wife because I already have one,' replied my husband quickly and sharply.
'Well thank you dear, I'm flattered, but why didn't you tell me earlier. We can just say this is our house, but I don't know what we are going to do about the furniture. We might be able to rent some from Cathy, remember her? She's my best friend,' I responded briskly.

All that night my husband Ian wouldn't sleep, all he did was watch television. It wasn't that bad was it, or did it mean that much to him?

The next morning I woke up to find Ian had left earlier for work. He must be so worried about tomorrow. I must do something and I know the perfect person to go to.

Ring! Ring! 'Oh come on Cathy, answer the door.' Ring! Ring! 'Still not there, oh well, I'll go to Melanie's then,' I said in a small whisper.

Ring! Ring! I thumped the bell fairly hard and quickly so I could get her attention. 'Coming!' Brilliant, I must have caught her before she goes to bingo.

'Oh hello Mel. Sorry to bother you, but I was wondering, would it be possible for me to borrow an ornament or a small painting or coffee table to smarten up my house with, as my husband's boss is coming over tomorrow and our flat is so horrible, please?' I whinged.
'Of course you can Julie. Come through, I'm sure I'll find something, Now would you like a painting or simply a beautiful ornament?'
'Oh anything, anything, thank you so much.'

I was then led through to a large airy hallway passing many lovely paintings, ornaments, drawers, desks and chairs, but then I spotted the most perfect tea set hidden away at the back of a small glass cabinet.

'Umm Mel!' I said quietly, 'would it be possible for me to have a peep at that tea set?'
'Which one? Oh that one. I inherited that from my grandmother. It was given to her by a duke because my grandmother used to be his head maid for many years and when she left he gave that gorgeous tea set to her,' Mel replied politely.
'How lovely,' I said. 'Would it be possible for me to borrow it though?'
'Oh yes, but please take care of it,' Mel answered.
'Not to worry, I will,' I reassured her.

That night I put up a few pictures I found in the cupboard and set out the tea set for tomorrow. I was pleased with myself, and so was Ian.

Knock! Knock! 'He's here Ian. I'll answer it,' I said as I hurried down the hall towards the door. As I opened it in popped a head.
'Hello, I'm Ryan, Ian's boss and you are Julie, am I right?' he said quickly.

'Oh yes I am. Would you like to come through to the living room and I'll call Ian,' I replied quickly, fairly amazed at Ryan because he seemed much friendlier than I thought.

'Ian love, Ryan's here,' I shouted.

'Coming dear,' he replied.

'Oh hi Ryan, I'm so glad you could come,' Ian said as he sat down.

'Ryan, would you like tea or coffee?' I called from the kitchen.

'Tea please,' he answered.

I walked slowly and carefully into the sitting room with the tea in Melanie's tea set. 'Do you like my tea set, it is very special, it came from a duke?' I boasted slightly lying.

'It's gorgeous Julie, if only it was available in shops, I'd love one for my wife.'

The meeting was going well until *crash!* 'Oh I'm so sorry. I would buy you another one if I could, really I would,' Ryan whimpered worriedly after he had just knocked the jug from the tea set over by accident, I hope.

'Not to worry,' I answered fighting back the tears as I cleared up the pieces of china and walked into the kitchen. I then sat down and randomly put the pieces of china back together, now crying as I couldn't fight back the tears any longer, when Ian walked in.

'Julie, are you all right?'

'Yes fine,' I said wiping back my tears. I'm not fine I was saying to myself as I walked back into the living room to join Ryan. What am I going to do? Melanie inherited that from her grandmother.

The rest of the meeting went well for Ian but I couldn't feel happy for him, the thought of the tea set stuck in my head, even when Ian got the promotion.

The next day I took a photo of the tea set and went shopping for something like the jug. I went searching in every china shop and I had nearly given up when I came to an antique shop on the corner of the high street. On a small coffee table at the back of the shop stood two jugs exactly the same as Melanie's one. I was so happy until I saw the price - one thousand, six hundred and fifty pounds. I couldn't believe it, but it was the only way out of this mess.

That evening Ian wasn't happy when I told him the price of the new jug. I took the tea set back to Melanie and she didn't suspect anything.

The next day I went for a stroll past the antique shop. 'Oh my God!' I said aloud, the jug was for sale for half the price.

Gemma Chambers (11)
Maltman's Green School, Gerrard's Cross, Bucks

MY BLACK BEAUTY

I had enjoyed my life in the large, pleasant meadow with a pond of clear water, but I didn't understand why I had to leave. Leave my kind owner, the large meadow and worst of all, my mother. I know I am older but it doesn't mean I won't miss her. After all, she was the horse who taught me all the things worth knowing. I enjoyed the times when the colts used to run around the meadow and I used to chase them. I shall never forget that wonderful farm. I never thought I would have to leave, but I know my life will change. I hope it doesn't, but I know it will.

I was beginning to get angry, stamping my foot and blowing loud raspberries. It wasn't fair! The other colts could stay, but why me? Why did I have to go?

Before I knew it, I was being walked out of those black, wooden gates I knew so well. I felt like stopping dead in my tracks and turning round, but I knew better than to disobey my master. Then I started to ask myself questions. If my new master is mean should I misbehave or should I behave? I didn't know which route to take. I began to think positively and thought, well that is not the way to go about the issue, so I started to think that my new owner would be a good owner not a horrible one.

I was then led through a narrow, rickety lane. I carried on walking along until I heard other horses, my heartbeat rose. Other horses, other colts? People talking? Was I being taken to the market? I answered my own questions with a yes.

Next I was led through some colourful banners. I had just entered the market where I was going to be sold. I began to get frisky, tossing my head. But then somehow I felt happy. Maybe it was because I had taken a step further in life, after all, I couldn't stay with my mother forever.

Other horses now surrounded me; some looked just like me, some were pure white and others were chestnut.

Later I was led into a small, cramped cubicle where people scribbled down notes about me and inspected every inch of me; they even looked at my teeth. I didn't think there was anything particularly interesting about my teeth! I counted eighteen people who seemed interested in me, but that was before they had seen the other horses. In the end two people came to talk to my master. Then, I heard one of them mumble something that sounded like, 'This horse looks too much like my other one, and he walked off. So now only one person wanted me. After a long discussion I heard my master barter with him.

'Three hundred and forty pounds, three hundred and fifty pounds, three hundred and sixty pounds, three hundred and seventy pounds. Sold!' My master said that was a good deal. So I had been sold for three hundred and seventy pounds. Somehow I felt strange.

I didn't know what was facing me, but I know I shall miss the past.

Taryn Dale (11)
Maltman's Green School, Gerrard's Cross, Bucks

THE THIEF AND THE BUSINESSMAN

'Thanks a bunch Mrs!' laughed Tony as he scurried away clutching tightly onto a black velvet handbag.

Tony wore a baggy T-shirt and fleece that blew fiercely in the strong wind that day. The hood of his fleece caught the wind and slowed down his speed. His face was unwashed and his eyes had deep wrinkles from lack of sleep. His straggly hair was greasy and dirty. He was a rather clumsy man who always forgot his black balaclava. It was a wonder that he had never been caught by the police.

He stole this beautiful velvet handbag from an elegant old lady who was just entering the clothes shop Alexon. It was about 6.00pm on a winter's night, an hour before The Chimes Mall in Uxbridge was to shut for the day. Tony had planned that the cover of darkness would hide his face so as not to be caught. He came up from behind and as the old lady shrieked, he stole quickly away grabbing tightly on to the handbag.

'Benjamin, hot casserole in the oven, come on!' shrieked Sarah as she heard the twist of the key at the varnished door of 66 Ballad Street in London. 'I say dear, it is rather nippy out there, it was chilly when I went to walk Pups.'
'Bad day, bad, bad day today, stock market has fallen again,' replied Benjamin, mumbling after each word.
'Oh you poor soul, coffee dear?' asked Sarah almost sarcastically.

Benjamin was a hardworking, high earning business man. Recently he had been looking really depressed. Occasionally he would have an extremely good day, come home in a wonderful mood and stroke their spaniel Pups. This definitely wasn't a good day.

A couple of minutes later he appeared in his casual clothes and went over to kiss his wife. He gave her a large hug and slowly walked over to his broad, mahogany chair at the head of the wooden dining table.

'Children, dinner and for heaven's sake don't trip over the dog,' said Sarah in what seemed such a squeaky, high voice it could be impossible.

Down the stairs came the three most darling children - one in her skirt and blouse, another in his dungarees and a baby in night-clothes, who was crawling. Once they saw Ben their faces lit up and their tiny lips broke into a smile. They ran to their father and the baby crawled over to him and laughed excitedly.

The next day, as he was walking past Hyde Park, Tony ran towards him and stopped exactly behind him. From across the street came running a podgy, stout policeman pointing a gun at Benjamin.

'Hands up!' said the policeman grinning at his own self-importance in the scenario. 'Anything you say will be taken against you in a court of law.'

Ben stared at the policeman in absolute terror. He was shell-shocked that a policeman could be arresting him, he had done nothing wrong. He started to turn pale green and fainted, falling heavily on the pavement.

The next thing he could remember was a cold, wet flannel being dabbed on his face. A blurry figure appeared and Ben immediately recognised it as the same plump, arrogant policeman he had met before.

'What was that for?' asked Ben obviously very annoyed.

'You see, we've been trying to catch this robber for months and I finally managed to,' replied the policeman proudly.

'Still no reason to frighten a fellow Englishman,' said Benjamin, extremely agitated by now.

'I've never had the chance to arrest someone with a gun. I wasn't going to make any exceptions just because a rich businessman showed up piggy in the middle,' snorted the policeman. 'Thought it was rather hilarious, never arrested a businessman.'

'Oh all right, have it your way, yes fine, giggle, but I'm suing!' replied Ben.

'You rich people don't need any more money!' shouted the policeman.

With that triumphant speech from Ben he stormed off to work at his office.

Katarina Kennedy (10)
Maltman's Green School, Gerrard's Cross, Bucks

A DAY IN THE LIFE OF DAVID BECKHAM

'Waaa! Waaa!'
'Brooklyn!' I shouted, 'it's eight am.' I got up and dressed for training.
I went downstairs. Oh no, not more photographers, I thought as I closed
the curtains. I had breakfast, then set off to training in my new £105,000
Aston Martin.

Sir Alex Ferguson gave us a really hard training session ahead of
tonight's match with Deportivo la Coruna. I then had an interview with
one of the Spanish press. We (the team) and Fergie announced the team
at a restaurant while having lunch. I was on the right of midfield with
Veron and Butt in the middle and Giggsy on the left.

Then I went back home and played football with Brooklyn till Victoria
went shopping, so I joined her. Afterwards I joined up with the team to
prepare for the match. We had a light snack at Old Trafford before
having a pre-match warm up.

Then the boss called us in for a team talk. That finished so we ran out
onto the pitch and lined up for kick-off.

We already had a 2-0 advantage from the first leg. After 15 minutes I
got the ball and Pedro Duscher came and took my legs off the ground.
As soon as I fell I knew I had a broken bone. I was stretchered off and
had an x-ray. My foot was broken.

I spent the night in hospital. I didn't know if I would be fit for the
World Cup, I didn't know if I would be fit for the European Cup Final
if Man U got there.

James Fox (10)
Morgans Primary School, Hertford, Herts

A DAY IN THE LIFE OF ME

My name is Kieran Taylor. I am 10 years old and I was born on the 27th October 1991. I go to Morgans Primary School and I am in Year 5. I enjoy going to school, but most of all I enjoy the weekends, especially Saturdays when the weather is warm and it doesn't get dark so early and I can play out until late.

On a Saturday I usually stay in bed until 10am because I don't like to get up early. When I eventually get out of bed I have a wash, get dressed and then go downstairs and have breakfast. My favourite breakfast cereal is Nestlé Cheerios. After breakfast I watch TV for a while and then I go out with my friends down to the park where we play basketball and ride our BMX bikes.

In the afternoon I go down the town with my mum and my sisters Melanie and Carley. If it is a nice day then we buy a McDonald's take-away and go to the Castle grounds.

When we have finished shopping we go home and I go back down the park on my BMX and hang out with the other children, either playing basketball or football and sometimes hunting for slow-worms.

When I go back home I have my tea and if it is still light I either play in the field near my home and we take a boomerang or my friends might come round to play in my back garden. If I don't feel like going back out then I play the PlayStation or go on the PC. I also enjoy building Lego models, and best of all because it is a Saturday and there is no school in the morning, I can stay up till late and watch a video. Then on Sunday I can have another lie-in.

Kieran Taylor (10)
Morgans Primary School, Hertford, Herts

A Day In The Life Of Harry Potter

Up at the moment the sun touches my bed, I hear owls coming to the castle from faraway lands, tooting their call with letters which contain loving words or sweets of all kinds to meet their owners inside the walls of Hogwarts School of Witchcraft and Wizardry.

Getting dressed for lessons, Snape is waiting to feel the gladness of taking house points, saying that I did something terrible and to turn Neville into a toad and then forgetting to turn him back.

Voldemort enslaving for my blood hiding in the great woods while drinking unicorns' blood is the only thing that keeps him alive, waiting for a chance when Dumbledore leaves the castle.

Malfoy with his sidekicks round him, waking the school with their silly jokes of me, 'Potter stinks' badges, selling them to all the boys and girls in the Slytherin's house. Wearing them to all the lessons inside the castle.

I wish I was normal without a care in the world, yet that was just a dream. For I am Harry Potter.

Tom Hardinges (10)
Morgans Primary School, Hertford, Herts

THE DIARY OF GANDALF GREYHAME

7th November,
I have returned from the depths of Moria. I have passed through water and I have passed through fire. I have battled the balrog until I am barely alive. But now I have returned after toiling for countless days, ever following the balrog, ever searching for light.

The day is with me now as I climb out of Moria and prepare for the last battle which songs will be sung about. It lightens my heart now to see fair Lothlorien on the horizon, for soon I hope to come to it. The lightning shall strike and the thunder shall roll.

I am the first to strike, but I have not done well for I am weak and weary from my hardships. The balrog though has done no better for I have wounded him badly. I thrust again at the monster of the depths and this time I aimed well and hit right. The balrog was hurt badly so I, Gandalf Greyhame, took another stroke. This time the balrog rebelled and I was forced to defend myself using all my power that was left.

Hereafter I cannot remember much except that it became much like a firework display. Very much the kind I did for Bilbo Baggins eleventy-first birthday party. What I do know is that Gwaihir the Windlord is carrying me to Lothlorien where I shall stay for a while to heal myself. Here I shall leave off for a bit until this evening when I shall write more.

I am thoroughly healed, though a bit put out, when I arrived here everyone was writing songs about my death which of course has not yet happened. Anyway, I thought they were quite good and its a shame that they are going to have to forget them for a while until I do really die. I had the most delicious feast though and Celeborn gave me a lovely surprise. Anyway that is all I feel like writing now.

Marion Wyllie (10)
Morgans Primary School, Hertford, Herts

A DAY IN THE LIFE OF A DOG

I'm a German Shepherd called Max. I have just woken up to my breakfast, a tin of succulent turkey. After about half an hour or so I go on a walk to stretch my legs and play fetch and obedience games. If I get some things right I get a treat. A kid was playing with a Frisbee and when it went in the river I went to retrieve it. The boy was happy when I saved his Frisbee, but my owner wasn't that impressed with me and when I shook water all over him, he went berserk. For that I would stay outside all night. Later on we went to the pet shop. The smells were lovely, I could smell pork, chicken, turkey and beef and loads of treats. We got some treats, tins of food and a lead because I broke the last one. We got home, I had a tin of beef and I got ready for a long, cold night in the garden. But it wasn't as bad as I thought because I had a kennel to sleep in. About one hour later I fell asleep uncomfortably.

Jordan Crabb (10)
Morgans Primary School, Hertford, Herts

A DAY IN THE LIFE OF WINNIE THE POOH

Pooh woke up. He got up and looked around. 'I think it is time for a little something.' Pooh went to the cupboard and got out the honey pot. 'Mmmm,' said Pooh, 'that was scrumptious,' he said smacking his lips.

Pooh got up and put his T-shirt on. When he had, he opened his front door and went outside. Pooh walked down the long and dusty path to the bridge. When Pooh got there he saw his friends Rabbit, Owl, Piglet, Tigger, Roo and Kanga, Eeyore and last, but not least Christopher Robin.
'Hello everybody, what are you doing?' said Pooh merrily.
'Waiting for you so we could play Pooh Sticks,' said Rabbit.
'Oh,' said Pooh.
'You did bring them, didn't you Pooh?' said Piglet.
'Why yes,' he said, 'they're just over there,' said Pooh. Pooh pointed at a pile of sticks close by him.
'Well pick them up and let's play,' said Roo, in a cheerful voice.
Pooh picked them up and rushed over to the bridge.
'Ready 1, 2, 3!' said Christopher Robin.
Pooh dropped his long, brown stick into the river and rushed to the other side.
'And the winner is Pooh,' said Christopher Robin, as if he was a commentator. They played Pooh Sticks lots of times and Pooh kept winning.

When they had finished playing they all went to Christopher Robin's house for tea (Pooh ate honey).
When they were going home Tigger bounced on Pooh. 'Hey buddy bear, do you want to stay around my house for the night?'
'Okay,' said Pooh.
When Pooh got to Tigger's house he climbed the ladder, leaped into bed, pulled the covers over, and fell asleep.

Adnahn Qureshi (10)
Morgans Primary School, Hertford, Herts

A DAY IN THE LIFE OF BRITNEY SPEARS

I woke up. Yawn! It was 5am. I got up and got dressed, put a bit of make-up on. I was wearing my posh French tracksuit. I went into the giant dining room for breakfast. First, I had a bowl of cereal, then some toast and then a few croissants and bacon and egg.

After breakfast I walked into the gym and my gym instructor was standing there. Suddenly he screamed, 'Go over there and start lifting weights.'

I ran over and started lifting weights. After that I did 20 laps around part of the grounds and lots, lots more. I collapsed on my bed exhausted. I got some words out from my drawer. I started memorising them since they were my script for my new movie Crossroads. Making a movie's hard, but it's worth it.

I called my make-up artist and I heard her footsteps pattering down the hallway. She started working on me as soon as she got in my room. My make-up was finished at around 9am.

I walked over to my ballroom where rehearsals for Crossroads were going to be held. I went into what was going to be my dressing room for the day. I saw my outfit hanging up. I got changed as quick as I could and ran into the gigantic room. Everyone was waiting. The lights shone on me. I started saying my lines and everything went smoothly from there onwards. Well, I did make a few mistakes, about three, but I wasn't really counting.

It was around 8pm when rehearsals finished. My chauffeur showed me to my limousine because I was going out to a trendy restaurant. It was just outside of town in a really quiet place so I wouldn't have to wear a disguise. It was really late when I got home. I just collapsed on my bed and fell asleep.

Caroline Barron (10)
Morgans Primary School, Hertford, Herts

A DAY IN THE LIFE OF A HAMSTER

I wake up and slowly pull myself out of my little house. It's still dark outside. Anyway, I climb into my wheel and start running. After a little while I go and have a drink.

Soon my owner came downstairs to clean my cage and give me some food and fresh water. I am taken out of my cage and put into my ball. Soon I am rolling around having a great time. Uh, oh, I've banged into the TV again. Finally my owner picks me up and gives me a morning cuddle. Now I'm back in my cage, I feel really tired. Right, I'm going back to bed.

Aarrghh! Great all the family have gone out. Emily my owner has left the cage door open a bit. Let's go exploring.

I'm out of the cage, I'm just heaving myself up the stairs, now whose bedroom should I go in first? I think it's going to be Mum and Dad's. Their bed's really comfortable. I'm sitting on the bed and I'm sinking in, I'd better get off.

I'm now in Emily's room, she's got lovely, fluffy slippers. I'm just going inside them. I feel all sleepy, I better get away.

'Mum, where's my hamster, Jasper gone?'
'Has he escaped again Emily?'
Uh, oh, she's coming upstairs.
'I've found him.'
'Where was he?'
'In my slippers.'
Poo! She's put me back in my cage, I better learn to just live with it. Goodnight.

Melissa White (10)
Morgans Primary School, Hertford, Herts

A Day In The Life Of A Hair Band

Hello, my name is Hattie; I'm a hair band. At the moment I'm in a box waiting for Florence to put me in her dark, curly and very knotty hair.

I can hear her coming. She usually has the same style. *Ouch!* She is pulling me, stretching me, I feel as though I'm going to snap. Although I'm her best scrunchey, when we go to the discos I bond with the other hair ties, we do have a good boogie together.

I hate it when she sprays all that hairspray on her hair. Well, she mainly gets it on me though.

We travel around hair band in hair band as hair bands do with their owners. At the end of the day, it's hair wash time and the hair gets released from my tight grip.

I got carelessly put on the side of the bath, I slipped. Ah, nearly down the plug hole, but Florence just saved me. That was a hairy moment. And soon my day comes to an end, she puts me back into my box. I slowly shrink back to my normal size. Goodnight.

Florence Kenny (10)
Morgans Primary School, Hertford, Herts

THE DEAD OF NIGHT

There's a graveyard behind the ruins of 24 Nightmare Column where the Wilberts used to live. No one ever goes there. The whole family is buried in the back garden. The Wilbert family have a grudge against Nightmare Column because in 1840 the Nightmare family won the vote to win the lane and they were competing against the Wilbert family.

There's a story that every night the Wilbert family and the Nightmare family come out of their graves at the stroke of midnight and they battle until the light of day. Also they say that every year on the date of the election, they fight to the death. So far the Nightmare family have won every time, but if the Wilbert family should win the fight, they will be able to stay out of their graves forever and haunt the village.

David Hansen (11)
Oakley CE Combined School, Oakley, Bucks

THE RETURN OF THE BARTON HALL GHOST

Vrooooom!

'Come on, line up here,' said Mrs Frogspond as the class lined up to get their keys for the room at Barton Hall, (the holiday park they were staying at). The coach pulled away leaving them there at the strange-looking place. 'Come on, you will miss out first activity. Quad Biking!'

'Yes!' everybody shouted.

While they were walking to the quad bikes, they heard rustling and it was cold. Everybody was scared apart from Tim and John, two mates that weren't scared of anything apart from ghosts.

They did all the activities, blind trail, abseiling and ICT. Then everybody went to dinner, after that they went to bed because they were tired.

In the night there was a thunderstorm. Everybody was scared apart from Tim and John. They heard a knock on the window and went to investigate. When they were walking down the stairs the chandelier was jingling, they weren't scared. The two boys were walking, when suddenly the trees were rustling. Almost immediately they swung around, saw the most hideous, ugly figure they had ever seen in their lives. They didn't know whether to run or hide! But they just stood there staring until the suspense was no more. They had to run, but the ghost was following, chopping an axe down as he came.

Suddenly the ghost just fell into thin air. They couldn't believe it; they just stood there staring in the hole where he had fallen. Then they walked back. Their teacher was waiting there. 'Where have you been, you two?'

'Ummm, to get a drink,' Tim replied.

'Well, it looks as if you've seen a ghost!'

Tim and John stared at each other!

The next morning they packed their bags because they were leaving. Their coach arrived and they got in. They couldn't wait to tell their parents, because they would be scared silly. Tim and John still think about the ghost, wondering about him, whether he is dead or alive?

Thomas Lloyd (10)
Oakley CE Combined School, Oakley, Bucks

THE TALE OF THE OLD TOY SHOP

Sam and Danny sat in front of the TV, their eyes transfixed on an advert. It was about a toy shop called Toys Aren't Us! The advert said it was spooky fun. 'Adults only, no children or else,' continued the advert. The two boys looked at each other, and then listened to the rest. 'Open Monday to Friday, 1 till 3.' Their faces fell. Well Sam's did.
'I've got a plan,' whispered Danny.
'Oh no, you've got that, I'm going to do something stupid, look in your eyes again,' replied Sam smirking.
'Just hear me out, ok,' demanded Danny.
'It's not like I'm going to lose an arm over this,' replied Sam sighing.

So the two boys sat down and listened to the plan. When Danny finally persuaded Sam to go through with it they celebrated with a can of Coke.

The first sign of the place being spooky was when the man on TV repeated the *no children or else* part about seven times! They went to bed that night with huge grins on their faces.

It was a Monday morning and Danny woke up startled to see he was in the toy shop, but the thing that surprised him most was the smell of rotten eggs. And the temperature changing; hot, cold, hot cold. He stood up and someone or something touched him on the shoulder. He turned round and saw the most revolting and ghastly thing you could imagine and worse! He was standing with a rifle in one hand and a laser gun in the other. Danny ran to the door, but the ghost yelled after him. 'Can't you read, *no children!*'

He shot Danny in the chest, blood splattered everywhere. Then it put a gun to Danny's head . . .

Danny woke up petrified. Sam and Danny walked to school together keeping quiet about their dreams. You see they'd both had the same dream. They got to school and did all the lessons they meant to do. At break time they silently slipped under the fence and ran to the toy shop. When they got there puffing and panting, they opened the door and immediately felt they were not alone. They decided to leave so they turned round, tried pushing the handle, but the door was locked.
'Hello,' said a deep voice.

The boys swung round.
'Awwwwwwwwwww children!'
'Frankenstein!' yelled the man.

As fast as lightning a thing in a black coat appeared. Slowly, very slowly, he lifted the hood away and shrieked the most ear-splitting 'Booooooooooooo' you could imagine and worse. Its eyes were red like fire. Its head was covered in cuts and sores. And his body had bloodstained bandages wrapped all around its body. It had the tongue of a snake and was like fog dimming in and out. Just looking at it made you think what an evil and spiteful thing it was. Sam ran to the door, but when he touched it all the lights went out. There was a shout and a scream. The lights turned back on. Had it been a dream?

But again they saw the ghastly figure with the head of a man in one hand and an axe in the other. He slowly started to advance towards them. He took a swipe, but hit the glass behind them and totally shattered the glass. The two boys jumped out of the window and ran. The two boys turned around, nothing. They swung back and the ghastly figure met their eyes. Danny ran, he heard a shout, he swung round and blood splattered his face, but out of the carnage he saw Sam back to Danny. His arm was dangling from his shoulder.
'Are you al . . . ?'
'Just run!' yelled Sam not stopping.
They saw a vacuum cleaner shop. Danny ran up to it and smashed the glass. He grabbed one of the vacuum cleaners and switched it on and sucked up the ghost. They started to celebrate, but heard a rumble and a smash. They turned round and shattered glass met their faces.

Jamie Durrant (11)
Oakley CE Combined School, Oakley, Bucks

DON'T GO THERE

'She used to be a teacher, that ghost of classroom three,' read Miss Williamson. I was shivering, as she did so I looked behind me. I felt something there. Nothing! What happened next I don't know, but I think I was taken somewhere, it was like a dream! I ran, not daring to look back. I did nothing. I kept running, not stopping. I couldn't help myself. I looked back once more and felt a sharp pain across my chest.

I woke back at school. Miss Williamson above my head. Blood by my neck as the cupboard opened. I collapsed, not knowing what would happen next. I thought I woke, but was not sure at first. I was back in the classroom. Nothing had happened, everything seemed solid as a rock. What was happening? I woke this time for real. I was still in the classroom, but not, something was different. I felt a cold, eerie presence around me. I moved away, scared to death. It was like a dream, but it was no dream.

I ran on a road that never ended, not wanting to look, not knowing what I was running from or to. No, this was different! I heard a voice, a high voice, it said, 'Erica, Erica, come and help me or I won't help *you.*'

Soon after I was back in the classroom, it was cluttered with rubbish and something invisible was emptying the bin. Suddenly the figure appeared. At first, just the outline, then it was a holographic figure. It became a solid figure, very pale like a young teacher, from about ten years ago. I glimpsed at her, but only for a second. Then it disappeared!

Once again one of the clay pots rose, whisked itself across the room and crashed down, as another rose, spun across the room through the window and landed on the grass outside. Something was different about the figure. The way it dimmed in and out, the way it moved like something was wrong. The figure appeared once more. I was terrified now. It wasn't the teacher, a black cloak with no face, just bone, no legs or arms, just hovering around the room swishing this way and that. It was looking for something. It looked in my direction and dived towards me. I was horrified!

I couldn't move I was stuck dead in my tracks. It lifted me from the ground and took me far away from school. I couldn't see where I was. Its hands were over my eyes. 'Ghost,' I screamed.

'I fell far to the ground back in school as the day ended,' read Erica.

Verity Hanson (10)
Oakley CE Combined School, Oakley, Bucks

COUNT RABBITULAR AND THE ZOMBIE VAMPIRES

It was a dark, cold, winter's night, the wind howled *whoosh!* The owls hooted, tu-whit-tu-whoo and if you listened carefully you might have heard a distant groaning. The groaning zombies make when they arise from the dead.

Kane sat up in his sleeping bag. 'I don't like this Rupert, the woods outside look spooky.'

'It's only a camping trip, what can go wrong?' replied Rupert.

Kane with his vivid imagination, thought about this and answered, 'Zombies, vampires, zombie-vampires,'

But he stopped because Rupert, totally ignoring him, said, 'OK, let's go and see then.'

They clambered out of their tent, it was pouring outside, they walked west and soon they came to a distinct groaning sound. The boys ducked behind a bush and moved a few leaves away, what they saw was horrific. It was a giant, floppy-eared Bunny!

'Aaaaaaaaaggggggggghhhh!'

It had pink fur all over its body and razor-sharp claws. It had a black cape draped over its back. There were scars all over his body and face, but his teeth were slightly different to normal, giant, floppy-eared bunny teeth because of two bloodstained, razor-sharp fangs!

Suddenly the ground rumbled and shook. About a thousand cracks appeared in the ground, they were just big enough for a man or zombie to fit through. Green hands were poking through the cracks and there was a very loud groaning sound coming from inside them.

Suddenly there was a very loud groan from behind them made by vampires and zombies mixed together.

'Vampire-zombies!' shouted the boys.

Green and mindless, scarred and scary was the only way to describe them. They advanced. Kane whipped out the garlic, but zombies don't mind garlic, so they kept on coming. The only way was to fight . . . or

'Run,' shouted Rupert.

They ran! The ZVs jumped to catch them, but they missed. Then the boys realised that the only way out was through the woods! They ran over the ZVs that had fallen, but one grabbed Rupert's leg and he fell with a crash, hard on the floor, the last thing he saw was Kane fighting his way through the ZVs.

It was early one morning when Robert awoke, Robert was tied to a giant, metal bar and was in a building, Vampires and Zombies Ltd, the company that makes vampire and zombie toys.
'So you are awake.' It was the giant, evil bunny. Name of Count.
'Rabbitular actually and yes I can read your mind, but onto my fiendish gloating about my plan, I was going to take over your world, but no thanks to you meddling kids, I'm going to just take over your town.'
'Hey, you said you meddling kids, so am I on Scooby-doo?'
'No, you're not, idiot! Why did I take an idiot for a hostage, why?'

Suddenly Kane burst in.
'Seize him,' bellowed the Count, but Kane was too quick for the blood-sucking zombies, he untied Robert and they left the ZVs in their dust.

When they got home the door was locked so they climbed the ivy into their room, but as soon as they got into their room they saw it was a trap! 'There were ZVs in their room and walking onto the front lawn.
'You know too much,' bellowed Count Rabbitular. 'Die!'
Was this the end? Killed at 10 years old by a giant, pink, floppy-eared, vampire bunny?

Rupert Pickering (10)
Oakley CE Combined School, Oakley, Bucks

THE HEADLESS GHOST

'I know a song that will get on your nerves,' sang the children of Class 4 at Blueberry school. They were on a bus, on their way to a day out at an old, abandoned village. They drew up to the old, squeaky iron gates. 'We will walk from here,' said Mr Garrison. As the class got out of the bus and got into groups.

They started walking. Jack and John were two best friends and they were in the same group together. John's shoelace came undone. They dropped behind to do it up and carried on. The small village with no more than 20 houses was very dark and gloomy and stank of dead things!
'Jack,' shouted John, 'come over here.'
John was gazing into an old barn.
'Wow!' they both yelled at the same time.

Jack and John went into the old barn; it had an old, tattered roof with holes in it. They stepped in and screamed. What lay before their eyes were heads, with blood splashing around on the floor. They heard footsteps in front of them and saw a shadow on the wall. There was a silence. A ghost jumped out from behind the boxes and said, 'Give me your head!'
'Aaaaahhhh!' shouted Jack. 'Run!'
As Jack and John ran out of the barn, they bumped into something, it was the ghost.

They ran, their lives depended on their legs. Then they got trapped in a corner. Alex, their friend came in and smashed the beast over the back. The thing turned around and sliced his head off in one. Then the ghost picked up Alex's head and threw it at John.
'Hey, be careful, you could hurt someone with that,' as he kicked it back to him.

They found their group and carried on walking with them. They didn't want to tell them because they thought they would think that they were silly. They were so scared and they wanted to go home. They stopped at the barn and John and Jack told them not to go in, but they went in and came out screaming. They ran after them finding it hard to keep up.

What is this ghost? What does it want from us? What have we done to him? thought John.

We have to find a way to fix it, thought Jack.

'We must kill him. But how?' asked John.

'We creep up behind him and bash him over the head with a piece of wood,' replied Jack. 'OK?'

'He hasn't got a head,' said John.

'Oh yeah,' said Jack embarrassed.

'How about we find a sharp object and stab him in the belly,' suggested John.

Jack and John set about trying to find a sharp object to kill him. They couldn't find anything at all. Then at long last they found something to stab him with.

They went back to the barn and hid behind a bale of hay. The ghost walked up to them. They stabbed him as planned. As he fell to the ground in pain, a flush of guilt went through them. Since that day they have always thought of the day when they killed that ghost.

Matthew Pickford (11)
Oakley CE Combined School, Oakley, Bucks

THINGS THAT GO THUMP IN THE NIGHT!

It all started on Saturday. Rupert was staying the night, because it was his sister's birthday and 11 girls were staying the night at his house. After playing on the PlayStation until 9.15pm we played chess, 4 games, I won them all.

By this time it was 11.30pm and I decided to retell the story Angus told us at school about Jimmy Walkgrove, who, on the stroke of midnight killed ten teenagers. He was put in jail, but escaped. The neighbours nicknamed him, 'Jumpy Jimmy' because, his trademark was a twitching left eye. Nobody knew what happened to him, but legend has it that every ten years, after he killed those ten teenagers, he kills again on the stroke of midnight.

'He killed those teenagers one hundred years ago *tonight!*' said I, as my watched beeped to mark it was twelve o'clock.
'Midnight,' said I.
'Want to go to sleep now Alex?' Rupert asked.
'OK,' I replied.

Rupert jumped into the bed on the floor and I got into my bed and jumped - when I saw my own reflection in a bloodstained axe. I looked up and saw a man with a madly twitching left eye.
'Chop, chop,' he said quickly.

Rupert jumped up off the floor, picked up a book. He was just about to bring it down on the man's head when the axe came down on Rupert's neck. The head hit the ground with a thump. I stood petrified as the body of Rupert found a new owner. The man crawled into Rupert's body.
'Ah, skin again, all I have to do is stay in this flesh for one hour, then it's mine. Oh yes, Jimmy's back in town,' said Jumpy Jimmy gleefully.
'Jumpy Jimmy,' I said under my breath. I looked at my watch - 12.16. Then I looked up again. Jimmy had a heavy book held over his head and he brought it down on my head. *Thump!* I stumbled. He raised the book again. *Thump!* I fell to the ground. I was barely conscious. Then *Thump!* I blacked out.

I came to when my watch beeped one in the morning. I opened my eyes. I saw Jimmy, axe raised! I rolled over. *Thump!* The axe hit the ground. I threw a punch at his ribs, he dropped the axe. I punched again; he looked up and kicked me hard in the shins. I punched again; he went mad and punched me across the room onto my CD player.

Jimmy retrieved the axe. I was momentarily dazed. He raised the axe. I jumped to my bed. He brought the axe down on the CD player. After a second pause, the CD player exploded, *Boom!* And it blew Rupert's body across the room. He hit the wall.

'What happened?' asked Rupert.

A ghostly figure came up from Rupert's body. 'I'll be back, you'll see!'

Alex Meakin (10)
Oakley CE Combined School, Oakley, Bucks

THE MASTER OF DESTRUCTION

'Yee-haa, whoo, that's so cool man!'
'Be careful Tim!'
Crash!
'Ouch, man that hurt.'
'Come on Tim, let's go home.'
'Yeah, OK,' replied Tim.

Susan woke up from the most pathetic dream she had ever had! She got
up, got dressed and went down to breakfast. Her long golden hair fell
around her shoulders like a golden curtain. 'Tim,' Susan said as she
came into the breakfast room, 'Hey, you ate the last of the . . . .'
She never did get to say what he ate the last of. *Bang, crash, clatter!* All
the plates smashed themselves against the wall. 'Ummmm, I don't think
we should go to the stomping ground today.'
'Ahh, come on sissy, you have always been scared of the skateboard
park!' he taunted.
'No, I have not,' Susan yelled indignantly.
'Well, come on then,' he said impatiently, dragging her along to the
stomping ground.

'Yee-haa,' Tim yelled as his skateboard wheels shot along the ground
crunching and spinning in the grave, faster and faster and faster. Until
eventually doing a double flip in the air, crashing, shooting out of the
skateboard park and rolling down the hill! Susan (who at the time had
been eating a sweet that she had found in her pocket), turned round in
surprise.

The wind had turned icy cold, Antarctica cold. She started to turn blue,
the leaves on the trees started rustling, the grass rippled under the trees'
firm roots and everything was quiet, deathly quiet. 'Tim,' Susan called
out sounding all quaky and scared. 'Tim where are you?'

Susan heard a noise behind her. She turned slowly rotating on the spot,
not wanting to turn, but she had no control over her feet, which seemed
to be attached to nothing. She finally came to look at exactly what was
behind her. It was a black, modern radio which had a tape recorded onto
it. The message said, 'You are the chosen ones, you have everything,
you will die!' Susan fainted.

Just at that moment Tim came up onto the crest of the hill carrying his skateboard. He took one look at her and put her on the skateboard. Afterwards she was surprised at how calm he was. Now if he had heard the tape maybe he wouldn't have gone down the alley with no people in it and gone the long way home, but he hadn't, so he did.

Tim was pushing the skateboard along when suddenly he felt as light as a feather. Suddenly he was as light as a feather! Because he was floating through the sky. He dropped like a stone onto a cloud. He looked up and then wished that he hadn't. As he looked into those dustbin lid eyes he shuddered, the distinct smell of rotting eggs came to his nose. The ghostly figure had silver eyes and you had the feeling they were powerful. His skin was green and knobbly. His nose was a metre long and crooked with corns on. His eyes were slits and his arms were long with gigantic muscles. His hair was long and brown just exactly like rats' tails, all long and brown and writhing! When he spoke his speech sounded like he had been sick and hadn't had a drink! 'I am the Master of Destruction. I am now going to kill both of you and suck the blood out from your heart. You are young and healthy, I need the strength.'

Suddenly Susan woke up and rolled out of the way just as the Master of Destruction brought the axe crashing down onto the skateboard. Tim grabbed a piece of the broken skateboard crashing down onto the Master of Destruction's head. The Master of Destruction yelled, screamed and died for the second time in his life!

We never did know what happened to Tim and Susan, but that little town was never the same again. Some people who lived near the outskirts of the town said they saw a little boy pushing a skateboard down a bumpy track and when they called to him he had gone!

Erica Smith (10)
Oakley CE Combined School, Oakley, Bucks

FANTASY ISLAND

Hello and welcome to Fantasy Island. I'm your host for the story and my name is Shinny. I'm a two-month-old unicorn and I have a brother called Spiral, my mother's name is Silver. I have got three friends, Goldey, Flyer and Grey Hair. Goldey and Flyer are sisters and they're phoenixes, Grey Hair is a werewolf. On the island there are lots of different species of animals like unicorns, phoenixes, werewolves, centaurs and things like that.

Today is Grey Hair's birthday and I can't think of something to get him! Never mind, I'm sure I'll think of something . . . I know what I'll get him, I'll get him a hairbrush.'

'Mum I'm going round to Grey Hair's house to wish him a happy birthday and give him his present, ok?'
'Yes honey, that's fine.'

Hi Grey Hair, happy birthday, here's your present.
'Oh hello Goldey and Flyer, I didn't see you there, how are you?'
'Oh fine thanks Shinny.'
'I'm having a party tonight, would you three like to come?'
'Oh yes please.'
'I'd better go and ask my mum.'
'Yes we'd better go and ask our parents too.'
'Be here at 5 o'clock.'
'Bye.'

Natalie Pearson (10)
Park Junior School, Wellingborough, Northants

STINKIN' SCHOOL WORK

I walk into school and hang around waiting for Sarah and Shannon. They arrive ten minutes after me, by that time, I'm in a rather tetchy mood but I am the great Tracy Magarath and I am not a stroppy person.

We walk down further into the playground and hang around there for a bit. Soon however, we see Mrs Shara coming out to blow the whistle. We dash over to the cloakroom door, the only person who manages to beat us is Emila Richards but out come our long pink tongues and off she goes sulking.

Shhhrrrreeeekkkk, the whistle goes and a line is starting to grow behind us. I feel a shove in my back and turn round, my tongue ready and see Emila just behind me, out comes the long, pink worm of a tongue and again off goes Emila.

I walk into the cloakroom and hang up my new, very stylish jacket. I walk up to the classroom and there starts a new very boring day.

Break time, I walk out into the playground and look round, I sneak off and climb over the fence, I was finally free forever.

Beth Williams (10)
Park Junior School, Wellingborough, Northants

THE MAGIC TUNNEL

Rachael was a typical girl of six. She had nobody to play with. She was bored. She decided to read a book. She picked up her book of fairy tales and started to read.

She suddenly noticed a small door with a sign on it saying *Say where to go.* She climbed inside and said, 'Please take me to Fairy Land.'

She blinked. She was in Fairy Land. Fairy Gemma came to meet her. Gemma took her on a tour. She met lots of fairies. She got to know lots of fairies and they talked about many things. There was one fairy Rachael liked most, called Maisie. Maisie liked Rachael too.

They talked late into the night, then one by one, they all went home. Rachael was so happy that she had made friends, but all of a sudden she was going back through the magic tunnel, then she was back in her bedroom.

Her book had finished.

But then, she swore she saw wings fluttering and felt Maisie land on her shoulder.
'Goodbye' she said.

Emily-Jane Richardson (10)
Park Junior School, Wellingborough, Northants

A JOURNEY TO MARS

I was playing with my friend Tom when there was a knock.

Zzzzzaaaaappppp!
We were floating in a humongous spaceship. Suddenly an orange alien came into the room. I asked him, 'Who are you?'
The alien replied, 'I am Marzipan and I come from Mars and I am here to ask you would you like to come to Mars?'
We both shouted, 'Yeah!'

So we darted past Venus and landed on Mars. There were lots of aliens thriving on Mars. Once we had played a game of Marsings and stuffed ourselves with Mars Bars, we came home.

'Ron! What was that?' I sat up in my bed. It was all a dream. My friend Tom was at my house. I said, 'Tom I've just had an excellent idea. Why don't we write a story about a journey to Mars?'
'Okay' said Tom.

So I wrote a story and Tom drew the pictures. Straightaway the story became a great hit. Afterwards, we took it even further and made a film. All the money raised was donated to the school library. To this day children are enjoying the most exciting books ever.

Priyesh Parmar (10)
Park Junior School, Wellingborough, Northants

THE SUSPENSE OF THE CRICKET PITCH

The sun emerged through the clouds. There was not a soul in sight! The pitch looked fresh and ready for the fantastic match! The audience were waiting patiently for the players to come out.

'Come on, come on India!' jeered the crowd. 'We know that you can do it!'

At that moment a group of people in white outfits came out slowly but steadily onto the pitch. Everybody stood up and cheered. Some of the crowd cheered for England. India cried, 'Boooo' to the part who supported England.

Suddenly there was silence! Not even a sound could be heard.
The commentator announced 'Today, the teams are India vs England!'

Sachin Tendulkar and Harbagan Singh were batting. Singh is known as the Turbinator because he wore a black turban. Caddick bowled at 80mph. Singh had hit a six and it went over the largest stadium in the entire world! Everybody cheered for India. All the drum players came out and drummed for India. India won the match so Harbagan Singh and Sachin Tendulkar turned out to the sports heroes of the game! India had won at last. What an amazing match it had turned out to be.

Nikul Kumar (10)
Park Junior School, Wellingborough, Northants

A DAY IN THE LIFE OF A FOX

It was six o'clock when I got up. I was very hungry so I went out hunting. I found a duck that was eating some seed on the bank. There was a bush behind him. I went in to it, shot out a claw and killed it. In pride I took it home and shared it out with my wife and two cubs.

I had my breakfast at 9pm since I am nocturnal. My parents live next door, so Sam and Hilary can go round and visit. My wife's parents live next door to my parents.
'Mark,' called Foxy.
'Yes love,' I called.
'Will you go and get the lunch?'
'Sure,' I said.
Here we go again, I sighed.

I went to the same place I found the duck and what a sight there was. I found the biggest, fattest, juiciest turkey I had ever seen. I jumped on it and killed it. I took it home and to my delight all of them were all ready for their supper.
'Hurry up and wash your hands, Daddy,' they chanted.

Tommy Hunt (10)
Sandon Primary School, Buntingford, Herts

THE SCREAM

It was the middle of the night. The door crept open. The lights went dim. The window kept on opening and shutting. I trembled. Then I heard a scream. It was a scream that made sweat run down my forehead.

I woke up in the morning and thought, perhaps it was all dream? I told my mum and she said that it must have been a dream because she and Dad didn't hear anything at all.

When I went to school, I told my best friend Louise about it and she said it was probably only a dream too. A nightmare.

When I went back home after school, I did my homework, had tea and went to bed. That night I didn't hear it, but the night after I did. It was the same cold scream that I had heard the night before.

The next day I went to investigate but found nothing. I wondered and wondered and wondered.

Two years have gone by now since I last heard that scream. I hope it doesn't come back. I guess that I never knew anything about it and that I never will, thank goodness! I wonder why it happened? Oh well!

Lizzy Hunt (10)
Sandon Primary School, Buntingford, Herts

PANIC

An old male pricked his ears, quite used to his surroundings. All the rabbits were safe from harm.

Below, in a burrow deep under ground, a fine doe called Saskia snuggled close to her five peacefully sleeping kittens. When awake the kittens seemed never to tire, only stopping to suckle. Saskia treasured these moments, smiling to herself in a content way.

A few hours later, the kittens awoke, Saskia tried to settle them again, but after struggling for some time she decided to let them play outside.

She sat at the opening of the burrow and watched her children frolic.
'Flopsy, Mopsy, Cottontail, Peter And Sienna' she mumbled to herself. She was distantly related to the famous rabbits children read about. Hence the names. But the last kitten, *Sienna* was her youngest and Saskia - although she wouldn't admit it - loved Sienna the most.

Thump, thump, thump. The oldest male was thumping his hind legs on the ground.

Rabbits appeared from everywhere bounding back to the burrows.
'One, two, three, four,' Sienna was nowhere to be seen!
Heart pounding, Saskia ran back to the burrow and sighed with relief when she saw Sienna. 'Never frighten me like that again!' she said.

Olivia Shaw (11)
Sandon Primary School, Buntingford, Herts

A Day In The Life Of Freddy

Hi! I'm Freddy the Ford Focus. It's a nice sunny day and I'm sunbathing on the driveway.

Oh no! Here they come. Looks like my sunbathing's over. Ouch! I wish they wouldn't throw things in my boot like that and if they slam the doors too hard, my sides will split.

I wish we didn't have to go so fast and these potholes make my wheels feel like they are going to fall off.

It looks like we are going to Tesco. I love talking to my friends in the car park, especially Patsy Peugeot and Thomas Toyota. I'm feeling very thirsty now, I hope they take me to the filling station.

I think we are going to the car wash now, it's great there. I love having my windscreen massaged and I especially like having my tummy scrubbed by that big machine.

I have got an ache in my engine at the moment, but I heard my owner say that I am being serviced tomorrow - so that should make it better.

Oh well, that's the end of another day, I just wish I had a garage to sleep in because it gets so cold out here at night.

Steven Musk (10)
Sandon Primary School, Buntingford, Herts

THE LIFE OF A JACKET POTATO

It has been quite nice in this rack. No one's been touching me. I have not been touched for five whole weeks. I am not going mouldy, but will go mouldy tomorrow. Yes . . . . yes, I'm picked. I get peeled and get put in an oven. I get hot and then I get pulled out and I have some cheese on me and I get put back in. I get out . . . and I get eaten. Haaaaaaaa!

Christopher Chandler (11)
Sandon Primary School, Buntingford, Herts

MY NEW SCHOOL

One morning I was going to a new school, when I got there I saw some lovely, kind children. The teacher called Mrs Spell seemed fine at first, when I got home, I went to sleep having bad dreams.

The next day she was deadly with me, my friends screamed at her but they knew they would get detention but they didn't, instead they were gone.

I was so desperate to scream, so I ran right outside (aaarrrggghhh!). What a nightmare. At last it was Friday, the worst day of all.

When I got in the classroom, everyone was muttering, 'Is this for real?' Then I realised Mrs Spell wasn't there, so I just joined in muttering. I saw someone who looked like her twin but more fashionable. I went to talk to her, she muttered and muttered. I was getting terribly bored, so I got someone's sock and put the smelly sock in her big massive mouth to shut her up.

Then Mrs Spell came back, my heart felt like an icicle, then I saw a wand. That made my heart beat faster than ever. It was going bo, bo, bo, bo, bo!

Then someone muttered to me, saying if you're looking for your real teacher, Mrs Spell, she's dead! We all found out she was a witch. We thought that was the end till now.

Lauren Osbourne (7)
Thrapston Primary School, Thrapston, Northants

MY STRANGE NEW DREAM SCHOOL

It was a blazing hot Monday, as hot as an oven, I was sweaty and I felt a bit sick. It was a little boring, besides it was my first day at school. All of a sudden I heard a terrible screeching sound. *Tttttrrrriiiinnnnggggg*! 'Oh no the bell, oh no not the bell!' I was nearly crying. I particularly hated the bell because we had to go inside and my teacher was horrible. She was called Miss Trunchney.

'Children come inside now!' She screamed from the other side of the playground. My teacher used to be a professional wrestler. 'You!' she shouted, 'what are you staring at boy!'

I was scared, I was rooted to the spot, I could not believe what she had just said. I felt all cold and shivering. I gasped open-mouthed. 'Are you a witch?' I asked worriedly.
'Yes, I mean, no!' she roared.

There were bits of blue all over her teeth. I ran. My teacher's eyes began to glow, I ran again but then suddenly I woke up. I was glad, it was all a dream, but what was that at my window?

Ross Munro (8)
Thrapston Primary School, Thrapston, Northants

THE TEACHER

It was my first day at school, I was very nervous and I was very excited too. Then I opened the front door, lots of children were looking at me and they were laughing at me too. Some of the children were throwing stones at me, then suddenly a voice was shouting from the other room.
'It's the horrible teacher!' said some children.
The teacher came out of the room, I stared at her and my heart was beating very fast. The teacher was wearing black gloves up to her elbows and a strange necklace. She looked at me and smiled too but I didn't smile back. Then the bell went ring and the teacher said, 'It's time to come back into the classroom.'
Everybody went rushing in and I said, 'Well she's a bit ugly as well' and I was standing in front of the classroom door. The teacher called me so I walked in the door. She was smiling at me again but I didn't smile back. I was shaking. We had a very long time for a lesson. It was lunchtime. When I was eating lunch, I met a new friend, her name is Lauren. She is very nice. After lunch we went outside onto the playground. Some children were teasing me but Lauren told me to just ignore them, so that is what I did. It was home time now. I went home and told my mum and dad that I was not happy at all.

It was the next day now and all of the teachers and children at school were nice to me so I went home and told my mum and dad and we all lived happily ever after.

Carmen Cheung (7)
Thrapston Primary School, Thrapston, Northants

MY DREAM

I was in bed fast asleep, I was starting to get a dream. It started off with me in my bed fast asleep, really cosy with my heating on. Suddenly a woman came into my bedroom with glasses on and ice and fire in the woman's eyes gleaming at me. Then she scratched her head and she walked to my bed. She limped closer to me, everything she wore was black. She put something over me and suddenly I woke up in a castle.

In the old castle, I heard people talking to each other, I thought they were noisy. I saw Grandma, I couldn't believe my eyes. I ran to Grandma who took me home.

The next morning it was real, the witch was in our home.
'Grandma' I said, but she couldn't hear me, then I went to her bedroom. She was not there. I looked everywhere for her. Downstairs, upstairs, everywhere, then I heard a voice in my head, it was saying she was at the old castle. My heart started to thump like mad, *thump, thump*!

The little voice was there again, I ran to the castle so quietly, I raced like the wind. When I opened the gate, Grandma was looking out of the window. I went in the house, I went upstairs, I saved Grandma and we went home.

Hannah Ward (7)
Thrapston Primary School, Thrapston, Northants

THE WITCH

One day after school, I walked home. The next day I walked back to school with my bag for the trip and my lunchbox. I got on the coach next to my friend. We got there at 10.15pm. Me and my friend went in the creepy, black castle.

Later we went walking up the stairs, when we heard this crash, bang, boom, wallop!

We saw a glimpse of black. We legged it upstairs to the tallest tower, we were trapped! We saw red, hot, boiling, baking fire pouring up the tower. We saw a black thing drive on a broom swiftly through the window. It froze the dragon and fire like a statue. The ugly creature exclaimed, 'You are lucky, I best come around with you because that was only a baby. There will be a mother and a father and more babies!'
'But who are you?' I exclaimed.
'I am a witch, a good witch!' explained the witch.
'But beware there is an evil witch around. I fought her many times alone and have always lost.'
'Ah ah ah ah ah!' echoed a voice.
'Oh no!' whispered the witch. Some woman just flew swiftly through the window so fast she was like a bullet. We could not even see her, she was so fast, she zoomed like a rocket down the stairs.

'Come on,' whispered the witch, 'quick, hurry before the dragon unfreezes!'

We ran down the tower, we were on the ground floor, we explored the castle until wwwhhhooossshhh! We were in a chamber. The witch said something, the chamber lit up all of a sudden.
Boom, bang, boom, bang!

'Here comes the father dragon,' shouted the witch.

The dragon was never seen again. As for the evil witch, she got beaten by the good witch so the good witch became a normal woman and everything was back to normal.

Jordon Mahon (8)
Thrapston Primary School, Thrapston, Northants

RUNNING AWAY

'Go James, go!' roared the audience.

It was sports day and James was one metre away from his opponent, the bully. James ran as fast as he could. Suddenly he caught up with the bully. Then he ran past the bully and when he was just about to run past the line, the bully's friend put a rope to his knees. He ran still but he did a forwards roll and landed on the ground. The school nurse came out of the school and picked James up.
She said, 'James, how did that happen?'
James whispered, 'Them two!' pointing to the bully's friends.

The bell rang and everyone went in to school. The school nurse and James went in to school. The school nurse and James then went to the hospital wing.

'Here have some food,' whispered the school nurse. James put the food next to him for later. The bully knocked on the door wanting to see James. The nurse opened the door and let him in. The nurse said, 'I'd better let you two be alone for a couple of minutes.'

When the school nurse had shut the door James' heart froze . . . the bully said, 'I'll beat you up for winning against me.'

James quickly ran out of the hospital wing. Then he ran out of the fire door, he ran into the forest, he slowed down and looked around and there behind him was the bully. He quickly started running through the trees and out the other side of the forest. He saw a tiger.

Suddenly a man came jumping out of a tree and James got on his back without thinking. The man ran into a hole in the tree. The man said, 'I'm an innocent robber, do you believe me?'
'I believe you' said James, wondering if he would see his mum and dad again.

George Clements (8)
Thrapston Primary School, Thrapston, Northants

MY NEW SCHOOL

One sunny morning at school, I was playing with my friends Ellie, Hannah and Molly. I was settling down at school ok. The next day our class went on a school trip to the seaside. Next, we played in the sea and we played with our buckets and spades.

This strange woman came up to us, we didn't know who she was. She went into the sea with her socks and shoes on, she was strange so we ignored her and went away.

Then when we got back to school, she started to disappear, I was feeling very frightened, so were my friends. My heart started to shake, she was like a ghost to me, then she fell flat on the floor. We were furious. We ran away as fast as we could at about 60 miles per hour. Then she was right behind us, we screamed, 'Run as fast as we can.'

We ran as fast as possible, she still caught up with us. We really tried hard, then we hid behind a rock, she didn't find us. We did not know who she was.

Georgina Reid (7)
Thrapston Primary School, Thrapston, Northants

MY NEW TEACHER

I woke up at 6am in the morning and my heart sank to the bottom of my tummy. I gulped, then I pulled my bedcover over me, Mum came in and looked at me. 'What's the matter?' Mum asked.
'Um, um I'm a bit scared,' I whispered.
'You're frightened,' Mum said surprisingly.
'Well yes,' I whispered to Mum.

I got out of bed looking so scared I felt like ice. I got dressed slowly and I dragged my clothes on the floor. I did everything as slow as I could. Mum took me to school in the car. When we got there, everyone stared at me. I went bright red. Mum was looking at me when the bell rang.

I walked into the classroom with Mum. My teacher looked pretty. She looked as if she was a kind, helpful, lady. She was called Mrs Davey. I had to find my peg. Then I started crying.

Once I had done literacy, it was ok and I liked it. I made a friend called Ellie and she was quite like me. Ellie hadn't been at this school for very long. My teacher asked me, 'How do you like your new school then Hannah?'
'Fabulous!' I shouted, 'I've settled in nicely.'

I made friends with Georgina and Molly. We did science next. I loved it, home time came.

Mum asked me 'How was your day then?'
'Excellent!' I shouted.

We went home. Next morning I came to school on my own and my teacher had different colour hair. She was acting very strange. She had a green drink. When she wrote and drew on the board, her writing was different. My friends' and my hearts were beating as fast as a cheetahs. Her face was going pale to dark red and she was talking completely different. I went darker red than the teacher. My tummy rumbled and I was so frightened.

My friends looked scared too. The day went very fast. Molly, Georgina and Ellie came home with me. We played in my back garden climbing trees. We pretended to be spies. I looked in my bedroom window and I saw my teacher in my bed. 'What?'

I told my friends, we all felt like statues. We ran up the stairs and into my bedroom. My teacher was laying on my bed with one of my books on her face, snoring. We waited and waited for her to wake up and when she did wake up, she stared at us and then she got out of my bed in her pyjamas and jumped out of the window and ran away screaming. We all laughed.

The next day she was so strange because her hair was sticking up and everyone laughed. At play time everyone crowded round and whispered 'What is our teacher? What is she?'

Nobody knew. We did numeracy but Mrs Davey thought it was literacy. Then we did science but she taught us numeracy. We did history but she taught us science. We were all very, very puzzled.

We went home. I said to my mum 'Everything was so strange today!'

Next morning I took a mouse to school. Ellie took a very unusual animal to school. My teacher shrieked - What was it?

Hannah Pendred (8)
Thrapston Primary School, Thrapston, Northants

IS MY TEACHER A WITCH?

Brrriiinnnnggg!
'Who is she?' asked Imi.
'Who is she?' I repeated. There sitting on the teacher's chair was not the normal teacher but a strange lady. She had black hair, blacker than coal, she was wearing a black dress with black shoes and her face was as white as a ghost. She had blood-red lips that forced themselves into a piercing smile. I wish she hadn't.

'My name is Miss Coal,' she answered. Somehow I didn't feel right so I went and sat down by my best friend Imi.
'Move,' came a shrill voice.
'What?' I said.
'Don't what me. Move,' Miss Coal repeated.
'Mrs Davey lets us sit where we want,' I argued.
'Well I don't and that's that!' Miss Coal shouted, 'now move!'
I had lost.

At play time Miss Coal made me stay in and write 'I will not be naughty' 50 times! When I finally got on the playground Imi had lost her skipping rope.
'I gave it to Miss Coal and she won't give it back,' sobbed Imi.
'Well don't worry,' I said trying to comfort her, 'she'll probably give it back in the morning, actually you'll probably wake up in the morning and find it was all a dream.'

In class Miss Coal pretended to accidentally lean on the light switch.
'Aaaggghhh!' screamed Imi. 'I hate the dark!'
I found the switch and turned the light on again.

When we went swimming Miss Coal made me go to the deep end!

In science Imi was playing with a balloon and Miss Coal came along and popped it, plus she gave me 50/100, how bad is that?

At home time Imi and I both saw Miss Coal scratching her head and then we noticed she was wearing gloves inside!

The next day we had our old teacher back (boy I was glad) but she had some very bad news . . . she was retiring and Miss Coal was taking her place!

My blood turned to ice.

Holly Anderson (8)
Thrapston Primary School, Thrapston, Northants

ME AND THE WITCH

'I don't want to go to a new school Mum,' I shouted
'It's quite spooky,' whispered Mum to Dad.

Here I am in my new school, my teacher looks peculiar. I didn't know anybody, I was scared, trembling with fear. All the children talked to each other but not to me. My teacher was bulky, rotten and a hideous sight. The next lesson was literacy and that was boring.

'Right get on with your work,' croaked the teacher in a dreadful mood. The problem was we didn't know what we were doing because she hadn't told us what to do. We had to work from five to nine until half-past six at night. We were very, very tired after we had finished school.

At lunch time she talked to me about how slowly I worked, 'Why do you work so slowly?' shouted the teacher.
'Because in our old school we had to work slowly, that was the rule,' I whispered.
'I don't care about your old school, I care about this school!' the teacher yelled at me horribly.
'Why?' I murmured quietly. 'My teacher is spooky after all,' I whispered.
Then the bell rang, all the children rushed into the classroom.

The next day I didn't go to school because I was ill and the teacher doesn't like children who are off school. I wasn't really ill, I just wanted to get away from that teacher for a day or two.

The next day I had to go to school to that horrible teacher again. I think because she is so horrible, she might be a witch. Next time I'll find out, I'll make a plan with my friends, so this is the plan.
'We will get a rope, a net and put a hook into the wall. We will hang the net on the rope and when I make a sign, you will drop the net on the teacher and we will pull the mask off the teacher and then we will have her.'

So we did and guess what we found? A witch.

We took her to the prison and locked her up but she had a wand and blew the door down and made a mess in the school. Soon she blew herself up and was never seen again.

William Gadsby (7)
Thrapston Primary School, Thrapston, Northants

MY NEW SCHOOL

I have just started at a new school and my teacher is acting very strange. I was nervous, my heart pounded like a steam train. I was trembling like jelly. A few days ago, she had walked into the door, today I stayed behind at school, she was sharpening a knife, I don't know why she was doing it. *Bang*! The door had slammed closed. It was the cleaner. I'd better hide behind the door. She didn't see me.

An hour later, I walked home and on my way, I saw my teacher driving home. I waved to her but she didn't see me. Hang on a minute that's not my teacher, my teacher's right behind me and she is following me home. She caught me and threw me in a sack. She threw me in the boot of her car. It was a ten minute drive in the car to my teacher's house.

Ten minutes later, I found myself in my teacher's knife compartment. She made me a slave for two weeks and 5 days. About halfway through my time of being a slave, she whispered 'You can have an hour break!' I think she's a witch.

An hour later, I came back from my break. It was teatime for her. Can you guess what she had for her tea?

Liam Carter (8)
Thrapston Primary School, Thrapston, Northants

MY TEACHER THE WITCH

Today I'm starting a new school. I'm scared like a horse. What happens if no one likes me? Mum said they will so I'll take her side.

My teacher's called Miss Dibaty, the name makes me laugh like there's a funny clown in front of me. Her voice sounds like a frog and a mouse put together. I'm not very sure about my teacher. She's a bit weird.

The bell went louder than a fire bell. I jumped out of my skin.
'Out you go class, time for break,' Miss Dibaty croaked. Out at break I met some friends, they were called Rhianna, Mary and Chelsea. I asked them about Miss Dibaty.
'People say she's a witch!' said Rhianna in a spooky voice.
'People say she can be really anxious sometimes.'

I started to wobble like jelly. 'Well is it true?' I whispered.
'Well let's find out,' yelled Mary, who's a bit lively and mad.
'Meet me in the tree house down the road at 4 o'clock.' Chelsea quietly grunted.

After school I went to the tree house. It got darker than a black horse. 'I've got it. Well you know they say in films you can kill a witch by putting water over their heads, why don't we do that?' I smiled.

We all agreed, so the next day when it was time for break, we got a bucket of cold water, colder than ice and tipped it over Miss Dibaty's head. Her hair went blacker than night, she started to melt like an ice lolly in the sun, all that was left were clothes and we never saw the witch again!

Holly Robertson (8)
Thrapston Primary School, Thrapston, Northants

THE WITCH

I ran to school because I was so excited. Mum called out to me, 'Come back, slow down!'
'No, I won't come back Mum!' I shouted.

My heart thundered like a parent knocking on the door.

It was pouring with rain, I got soaked. Bang! A big, huge blast of thunder filled the air. I charged like a horse getting shot. I stuttered, I was getting closer to the school. I was going to have a new teacher. A car swerved around the corner. I was just about to cross the road when I stepped forward and my foot got run over.

The person in the car was my teacher. She laughed that much she fell out of the car. She ran to open the school gates. The caretaker opened the school gates instead. My teacher charged into school, then the children followed her even me.

She sounded really cruel. When we got something wrong, she would tell us to go outside and give us hard work.

I decided I did not like her.

Paula Dobson (8)
Thrapston Primary School, Thrapston, Northants

A WITCH TEACHER!

'Morning Sophie,' yawned Mum as she opened the curtains. 'Today you're going to your new school,' she said happily.
But I knew that meant trouble.

It was a sunny day. My brother Jason and I, Sophie, had settled down quite nicely. The school was smart, fresh, dazzling and joyful. Until that very moment when I saw her, my teacher, Miss Fangs!

I thought she was ugly, wicked, horrid, evil, smelly and cruel all because of her name. But that wasn't all, she had pale skin, frozen eyeballs and then, something caught my eye; she had wings growing out of her arms! 'Get out on the playground now!' she boomed.
As soon as I got onto the playground, the children, well most of them, were skipping. A girl called Lucy came to me and she became my friend.

We were skipping, then she just stumbled back into the school. I followed on. Every single child was saying, 'Fabulous teacher.'
Jason and Lucy came up to me. 'Thank goodness you're alright!'
I gasped!
'Every lunch time,' whispered Lucy, 'Miss Fangs goes to the National Olympics!'
'What, so you mean she's just been now?' I asked.
'Yes!' shouted Lucy.
'Right, I've got a plan,' Jason said excitedly.

We got a huge, marvellous bucket of water and tipped it over Miss Fangs' head! It melted her completely! We found out she was a witch! The spell that she did on the children was broken.

Mrs Coolned walked in, 'You are having Mr Blood Flooding from now on.'
'Oh no, not another problem!' I gasped.
'What if he's a wizard?' Jason asked with a scared face.

Rhianna Polson (7)
Thrapston Primary School, Thrapston, Northants

SPYING ON A WITCH

Suddenly Mrs Mawdsley tapped me on the shoulder. My blood was running to my heart! I was dragged to the bookcase! Mrs Mawdsley cackled, '*Abbyfromi.*'

A minute later, the bookcase opened up. Inside was a vast room. It had everything, a DVD player and a PlayStation 2. On the wall was a broomstick. I looked at Mrs Mawdsley, she was wearing a black leather top, it was black as coal. She was also wearing a necklace with a diamond witch on it, just like herself. She had a blue wool wig. I saw a blue bald head. She was shaking her head to try to put the wig on.

An hour later I was playing Scrabble with Mrs Mawdsley. She told me about herself. Mrs Mawdsley took one person a day. But one day she went to the head teacher, Mrs Holly Vindictive, to take her!

Taran Dulai (7)
Thrapston Primary School, Thrapston, Northants

WITCHES

It was a new world, a new school for Emily. She loved it there, but there was one thing wrong, the teacher looked like a witch. Her hat was as black as coal. Emily's legs trembled like jelly. She looked like an ordinary person with ordinary shoes, with an ordinary job, but she really did look like a witch.

It was extraordinarily marvellous and fantastic, but Emily tried not to laugh. Emily managed to get on with her, but she looked funny.
'Well, what an extraordinary person,' someone whispered from behind. Emily was a bit jealous at first.

The room was full of plants. It looked like a jungle because there were model tigers, but there were other jungle creatures too. She didn't like it.

It really now did look like she was a witch, because she had black hair, but it wasn't ordinary black hair, it was fluffy black hair, like a cat's. I asked her what her name was and she said, 'Naomi, witch, terrifying witch.' Her eyes looked mushy like mushy peas. Then all of a sudden there was a loud bang. Suddenly . . .

Emily Kelly (8)
Thrapston Primary School, Thrapston, Northants

WITCHES

I found I was in a new school. I was scared. Nobody knew me. I went to a little girl and the girl looked shy. I said, 'Hello.' She whimpered hello back. I asked her what her name was, but she did not reply. When I went into class I saw a shabby lady.

Then a boy came and he said quietly, 'My name's Robert.'
I muttered, 'My name's Cameron.'
'That's a fandabbydozy name,' he replied.

The next day I saw the shabby lady again. She was our teacher. She spoke funny. It sounded croaky.

I liked Robert. I sat next to him in class.

A week later I noticed something strange about the teacher.
She croaked, 'Stay here after school.'
So I did. It was only me and her.
'I'm a witch!' she screamed.
I was trapped, there was no escape.

Cameron Glynn (7)
Thrapston Primary School, Thrapston, Northants

THE TEACHER WITCH

It was my first day at school and my teacher was acting very strangely. I was very frightened and I thought she was a witch because she had gloves on. I was trembling with fright. I saw that she had a wig on.

Suddenly she was scratching the back of her head. I was shocked, she was a witch! I was trembling, my heart turned to ice. She looked bloodthirsty, she was staring at me straight in the eye. She was walking towards me. My legs were shaking. It was horrid. I could not stop shaking. Just then she looked at my work. Then she turned away. Do you think that she really was a witch? Decide for yourself.

Tristan McCarthy (8)
Thrapston Primary School, Thrapston, Northants

THE WITCH TEACHER

On the darkest, stormiest day, it was Joe's first day of school. Joe felt nervously excited. Loads of new friends will be there, Joe thought.

When Joe got to school, he was surprised. How many friends? At least eight. Everybody said hello to Joe and said their names. There was Billy, Amy, Tom, Alex, Hannah, Madaline, Andrew and Holly, but there was the mean teacher, Mrs Hipps. Do you know why she was called Mrs Hipps? Because she always had her hands on her hips. Joe was trembling like a leaf.

It was time to go into school. Joe found out that Mrs Hipps was wicked, sneaky, vicious, poisonous, snivelling, evil and ugly. When Joe got home he had cheese and tomato sandwiches.

The next day was Tuesday.
'Oh no,' Joe said cautiously.

At school, the teacher was acting strange. First, she put her head down the dustbin, secondly, she put her head down the drain.
'She's acting strangely,' Joe whispered to Billy, Amy, Tom, Alex, Hannah, Madaline, Andrew and Holly.
'Yes,' they all whispered back.
'She might be an alien from outer space,' shouted Andrew.
'Nah,' whispered Hannah, 'probably a witch.'
'Okay then, a witch,' shouted Joe.
'We'll spy on her,' Alex shouted.

At play time, they spied through a window. She was just drinking her tea. Then every dark night they crept into her garden and peered through the drainpipe into her bedroom. Then they saw her. She was a witch!

Very fast they galloped like a horse in the wind to the police station, but before they knew it, the evil witch was far, faraway. They went into the police station and told them everything, but they were too late. They went looking for miles and miles around. They could not find her. She had gone. They walked on, but on a wall there was a dark, dark shadow . . .

Thomas Cribb (7)
Thrapston Primary School, Thrapston, Northants

THE NEW TEACHER

Suddenly I realised I was moving to a wholesome school, with more children in it. It was what I really wanted. I had been begging and begging to go to a better school. My other one had green lumps over it. Inside it had squashed, juicy, crispy coleslaw everywhere! It was disgusting.

I felt really happy inside. My heart was beating with excitement, like a steam train going to blow up!

The next day was a dazzling, stunning day. I am never going to forget it. I was going to move schools. My dad took me in his fast sports car, because I wanted to get there before I counted to ten!

I was there. It had green ivy with a strange creamy middle. I was really joyful. I went to the classroom. On the desk it had a drink with green water, snail slime and a lump of snot. My teacher had big, gurgly eyes with a nose bigger than a clown, lips like an elephant with green camouflage. I knew this was going to be the end. It was so terrible. The teacher is really ugly, but I hope she is nice.

The next day I was at school, the teacher grabbed me and I couldn't get her off.

Hannah Gardner (8)
Thrapston Primary School, Thrapston, Northants

A DAY IN THE LIFE OF MICHELLE

Dear Diary,

This morning was a nightmare! Little Gari got up late and was late for school. Megan was sick all over my new wooden floor. I looked round and the dog had messed up the house and was lying in a wet patch!

Once Gari had got to school, thanks to Mick that is, I had to get dressed and I had to get Megan dressed too. While Gari was at school I got all my housework done. It looked really clean but wait until Gari walks in! He just jumps on the sofa and stays there all night whilst he watches cartoons.

I made dinner but burnt it just a bit! I still ate it though.

When we finished our dinner I put Gari and Megan back to bed. Soon after, I went to bed exhausted.

Kayleigh Dodd (11)
Victoria Junior School, Wellingborough, Northants

A Day In The Life Of Jimmy Neutron

Dear Diary,

My mum told me to smarten up my crazy hair, but I like it how it is. It suits me. I'm still working on a present for my mum's birthday. I've got it! I've invented the world's first colour-changing lipstick which doubles as a dancing ornament.

Had to run down to the comic bookstore. Problem: the cartoons are coming alive. It could be the work of those aliens again! It was really funny to see the comic book cartoons muck about, but I had to destroy the aliens and put the cartoons back. I did it, I saved world peace. As a reward, they gave me 1000 comic books featuring my favourite cartoon character, Jimbo and his gang. Oh no! Got to get home for dinner. Yuck, stew, but for desert, chocolate cake, made especially by Grandma.

Mum loves her presents. I'm getting sleepy. Write about the solar system for homework tomorrow . . .

Katherine Howford (11)
Victoria Junior School, Wellingborough, Northants

A DAY IN THE LIFE OF LARA CROFT

'Hello, Lara Croft speaking, who's calling?'
'Morning Lara. Albert speaking. We need your help. The Xian Dagger is trapped in some ruins in the African jungle near Somalia. The Concorde is waiting for you.'

Three hours later the Concorde landed and I jumped out. Waiting for me at the airport were guns and medipacks, also a monster of a jeep. So I drove to the jungle ruins and quickly ate my cheese and tomato sandwiches. I finally found the hidden door behind some ivy!

Beep, beep! The radar showed I was getting nearer to the Xian Dagger. My eyes spotted something glinting in the sunlight. It was the dagger. I picked it up, I felt hot breath on my neck, I spun around, dreading what I was about to see.

The creature was the size of a bus, with sparkling red scales, long golden talons, huge horns and rows of sharp teeth. It was a dragon! The dragon took a swipe at me but missed. As it crouched low, I grabbed the Xian Dagger and stabbed it in the heart. It let out a long piercing roar and crashed to the ground. Mission accomplished!

Siân Higlett (11)
Victoria Junior School, Wellingborough, Northants

MARGE SIMPSON

I woke up, had a lovely *cold* bath because Homer hadn't fixed the heater, then I got dressed, went downstairs and started to make breakfast. Four sausages, four rashes of bacon, five potatoes, fifty mushrooms, three fried eggs and two fried tomatoes for Homer. Me and the kids had the usual.

After breakfast, Bart went out and Lisa helped me with Maggie. Homer woke up and ate his breakfast. He wanted more so I cooked him four pork chops, three lamb chops, two plates of chips, donuts and beer.

Homer went bowling; Maggie woke up so I put the television on. Lisa went to the library. I made some sandwiches for lunch, then I started spring cleaning. Homer came home and invited everyone to a barbeque. At last, the chance to relax. I sunbathed for 30 minutes, but forgot the sunblock! At last they went and Homer went to Moe's.

Lisa came home with some books and Bart came home with a black eye. I made dinner then put Maggie to bed. Bart and Lisa went to bed after an argument. Homer hasn't come home yet, so I'm going to bed!

What a busy day . . .

Chaniece Pope (11)
Victoria Junior School, Wellingborough, Northants

A DAY IN THE LIFE OF VICTORIA BECKHAM

What a day!

I got up and fed Brooklyn, then woke David. Later I went to the studio to record my new song and shoot a video. That went quite well. Brooklyn was asleep.

Oh my gosh! Would you believe it, I just felt my first kick by the baby, but sadly, David was elsewhere.

I took Brooklyn shopping and brought some clothes for my baby girl I'm expecting. Went to the Argie Bargie for lunch. It was delicious!

This time David was so happy when I had another *kick*. Then it was time to watch David play football! Brooklyn was so excited he even joined in, and he scored. I left Brooklyn with David.

Then David rang to say that he had broken his leg. I picked up David and Brooklyn and David had to phone Sven and Fergie. They weren't happy either. We had dinner, then went home.

What a day!

Chantae St Hilaire (11)
Victoria Junior School, Wellingborough, Northants

A DAY IN THE LIFE OF THE FRESH PRINCE OF BEL AIR

I was woken up by my brand new thunder chunky alarm clock, which shocks and deafens you! I took one step down the stairs and I found myself on the bottom of the stairs in under three seconds!

My parents asked me what I wanted for breakfast, but I could not answer because I could not hear them.

I went to the cinema and I brought my dog along to watch Snow Dogs. Later on I went to a place called Burger King to get a burger. I dropped my father's teeth off at the dentist because they needed to be cleaned. I went to the shop and I met my friend, Jazz. Oh, she can play Jazz music well.

I went for a bath and it was boiling hot, so I jumped into our swimming pool and it was below -50°. After my action-packed day, I went to bed. Oh the relief!

Graham Pettitt (11)
Victoria Junior School, Wellingborough, Northants

A DAY IN THE LIFE OF DAVID BECKHAM

I was woken by Brooklyn bouncing on the bed. I took Brooklyn off the bed. I put my sharp suit on, then my snake-skinned shoes, given to me by Steve Irwin. I walked down the stairs on the boring, expensive carpet, our banister is all carved.

Victoria was moaning about how she put some weight on. Then I had some breakfast.

Later I went for a jog. I broke my toe. I cried.

I sat watching Mickey Mouse. I had lunch in the poshest coffee shop. I went shopping, I was on about my bank balance going down. Victoria could have bought the shop. We had to get a cab back. Sven phoned me about training, but I couldn't go because of the broken toe. Brooklyn was kicking me because he wanted to play football.

Victoria made some snacks. Then I played Fifa 2002 on my PS2. I had my dinner with Brooklyn and Victoria. I said to Victoria, 'My foot is feeling better, I'm taking the dog out.' The dog bit my toe so I went back. I went to a nightclub limping. I met up with Paul Scholes but he was drunk already.

Marcus Coles (11)
Victoria Junior School, Wellingborough, Northants

A DAY IN THE LIFE OF SALEM

7.45am I went downstairs and ate a breakfast of catnip and fish, then Sabrina carried me in her rucksack. She may not have known it, but she was helping me *try* to take over the world. She met Harvey, the perfect guinea pig for my plan to take over the world. With a mighty roar (squeaky miaow) I fell out of Sabrina's rucksack. I must have banged my head or something because something knocked some sense into me.

It isn't very nice when reality comes flying at one of us cats, it makes you realise you're a looser, idiot, prophetic. A cat later, I asked Sabrina to take me to the witch's council. I'll be blunt, she didn't let me so I cried and cried.

Then it hit me. I sneaked through the closet and paid the witches' council a visit and asked for another chance. They said they would put me on trial tomorrow. I have got a second chance.

Until then I'm going to relax, eat and gloat, then finally sleep. If only my old partners for the world domination plot were here to see this. Hold on, that gives me a good idea . . .

Luke Watts (11)
Victoria Junior School, Wellingborough, Northants

A DAY IN THE LIFE OF HARRY POTTER

I was woken up by Ron talking and screaming his head off in his sleep. I got out of my bed and went to brush my teeth. I then got changed into my black robe and woke up Ron and hurried to get downstairs.

On the table for breakfast, I ate bacon, chips and toast. I met Hermione who was eating. Professor Dumbledore was sitting on a high table to eat his breakfast.

Later on, I went to Snape's class for learning about potions and Hermione sat next to me! I wasn't paying attention so Snape took some points off. I thought Snape was horrible and nasty.

Afterwards, I went out as the lesson was finished. We played games as we went out of the classroom. We then realised that we were late for flying lessons, so we ran!

We had fun flying on our broomsticks and I was riding on my *Nimbus 2000*! Out teacher was Madame Hooch.

This was the day and we played Snitch against *Slytherin!* It was a tough game and in the end it was even tougher, but *Gryffindor* won! *Amazing! Wonderful!*

We won!

I won!

Krishna Patel (11)
Victoria Junior School, Wellingborough, Northants

A Day In The Life Of Homer Simpson

I woke up because the bed broke and Marge slapped me and I thought, doh. At least there was no work to do at the power plant.

I had a shower and shaved, then got dressed in my usual white T-shirt and my blue trousers that reeked.

Afterwards, I went downstairs and had the best breakfast ever - fishsticks with Duff beer and more Duff beer!

Then I went to the Kwik-E-Mart and bought: ten blue dyes for Marge's hair, five tubs of ice cream, some Duff beer, chocolate and a maths book for Lisa.

A few minutes later I went home to give Marge her hair dyes and Lisa her maths book. While I was at home, Bart took a tub of ice cream, so I chased him and strangled him until he gave me it back.

In the afternoon, I went to Moe's bar to have some beer. I ended up having too much, which I couldn't pay for. Moe threw me out into the street. Ouch!

Later that night, I went home and turned on the TV. I had some cheese for dinner because Marge was sleeping upstairs. I went upstairs and went to sleep on the floor with no covers. I woke up in the night feeling frozen and I said, 'Doh!'

Dishant Patel (11)
Victoria Junior School, Wellingborough, Northants

A DAY IN THE LIFE OF ANNE ROBINSON

I was woken up at 6.00am by the sound of the stupid alarm clock. I got changed into one of my many black suits.

I went downstairs and had my breakfast - eggs, bacon, beans, toast and orange juice. I watched a bit of television before I left for the photo studios. I did a photo shoot for 'Now' and had an interview with OK Magazine.

Later I went shopping in London and I bumped into Ruby Wax, so we had lunch together and talked about our TV shows. I went to Harrods and bought seven black suits and five pairs of shoes. I headed back home. I spent way too much money, but after all I am a TV star!

When I got home, I got ready to go to the BBC Television Studios. There I met the seven lucky contestants who were going to be on my famous show, 'The Weakest Link'. I wondered which one I would get a bit of backchat from.

When the show was over I returned home. I had fun today - I made one lady cry, embarrassed a man about his bald head and one contestant ran out of the studio screaming.

What a perfect day!

Jasmine Heath (10)
Victoria Junior School, Wellingborough, Northants

A DAY IN THE LIFE OF PRINCE CHARLES

My servant woke me up at 8am with a nice cup of tea. I asked my servant to run my bath, took my crown off and had a bath.

I had breakfast with my mummy, the Queen. Had Cheerio's, then went for a walk in the garden and spoke to the plants.

Later I met some people who were important. I signed some papers, giving lots of orders, then had coffee with Mummy and my sister, Princess Anne. Afterwards I opened a museum, boring!

Later I had lunch at McDonald's. I told them who I was and they gave me a free meal. I went to town in my limousine and shopped at Harrods. I spent a lot of money but put it on my credit card.

I came home and needed a rest from shopping. I went swimming for two hours until my skin went wrinkly, then had tea. We watched Teletubbies. I said goodbye to Mummy. I watched The Tweenies with Prince William and Harry, then we all started to play football in the garden and broke the royal window. Whoops! We had dinner, then went to bed.

Vinay Kapoor (11)
Victoria Junior School, Wellingborough, Northants

A DAY IN THE LIFE OF . . .

I was woken up by my owl, Hedwig, screeching in my ear. Ron and I dashed down to breakfast.

Then I had my potions lesson with Snape. When I was making my potion it blew up Malfoy's cloak, I was in big trouble.

It was then lunchtime. I was so annoyed with myself because I was not going down to lunch, even though it was my favourite dinner. I just ate what was left in my pocket and that was chocolate frogs and other yummy snacks!

Ron and I went up to the boys' dormitory. I had to get ready for the Quidditch practise. When I got to my bed I saw a parcel. I unwrapped it as fast as I could. I couldn't believe it, it was a Nimbus 2000!

Next I had my Quidditch practise. I quickly got the hang of it. Oliver gave me the position of being a seeker, I was so proud of myself. Ron was so pleased when I told him.

At 7.00pm we went to the common room. Hermione started on her homework as usual. Ron and I played chess, it was fun.

We went to bed, I was so happy, but I also felt exhausted.

Jemini Patel (11)
Victoria Junior School, Wellingborough, Northants

DAY IN THE LIFE OF SABRINA SPELLMAN

Firstly I was woken up by the sound of Salem shouting in his sleep. I had a shower, zapped myself dry and then put some clothes on. I was in a rush to get some breakfast; one piece of toast and some orange juice. I said goodbye to everyone and walked to school. I met Harvey on the way.

When I got to school, Libby called me a freak again and I got detention because I slammed my locker door. Mrs Quick taught me maths but I didn't listen. I had a talk with Mr Craft because I was not listening in maths. Then I went to science class, but I listened. Lunch time, I think it is the best time of day, but not today. I hate it when Harvey accepts to do something for Libby. He is my boyfriend, not hers.

I had biology and got a note from Harvey saying, 'Meet me after school at my house, I have a surprise for you'. I went straight to Harvey's. He kissed me on the cheek and we ran into his house. I was astonished. I went to sleep feeling really happy.

Lorraine Sebastian (11)
Victoria Junior School, Wellingborough, Northants

A DAY IN THE LIFE OF DAVID BECKHAM

I was woken up by Brooklyn punching me to get him some food. I had eggs, bacon, beans and toast for breakfast. Then I washed up and lay down to watch TV. I then got changed into my suit and shoes.

I went shopping with Brooklyn and Victoria and I thought Victoria bought way too much.

I went for a jog and got chased by a dog.

I had some sandwiches and watched cartoons with Brooklyn and I thought they were so funny, I almost laughed to death. Victoria called me a big baby.

I went training with the England squad and I ran so fast down the side of the pitch, I ran into the corner flag.

I went home and went to sleep. Then I woke up and played football with Brooklyn, he beat me 12-0.

I made me, Victoria and Brooklyn some snacks and Victoria blamed me for not getting her favourite cheese.

Then I played on my Xbox. I did some exercise and took the dog for a walk down the street.

I met Gary Neville and Paul Scholes at a restaurant to have a meal.

Tyrone Roach (10)
Victoria Junior School, Wellingborough, Northants

A Day In The Life Of . . .

I rang the bell for service in bed. I went into the bathroom and got changed into a purple dress and carefully put my crown on my head. Soon after I took the dogs (Corgis) for a walk. Straightaway when I got back I had a lot of important letters to sign.

I then polished my crown. I met with my secretary. Afterwards I spoke to Tony Blair on the phone and told him off. I went to McDonald's for lunch and had a Happy Meal.

I polished my crown again, then I went out and groomed my horses and went for a ride down The Mall. My servant followed behind me with a shovel.

I spoke to my secretary about the Jubilee arrangements then I went to tea with my son. I think I might have my tongue pierced like Zara.

I tried on all my jewellery and polished my crown again, then I got ready to go out on the town. I had a kebab and went partying around town. Finally I got in and fell asleep.

Teri-Anne Fisher (11)
Victoria Junior School, Wellingborough, Northants

A DAY IN THE LIFE OF

I get up because Harry and Ron are knocking on the door.

First lesson is potions with Snape. Why does that teacher always ask the other children and not me? I know *all* the answers! He would even prefer to ask *Seamus!* The other day he tried to make rum but ended up blowing himself up.

My next lesson is flying with Madame Hooch. She is a good teacher because she keeps everything simple, especially her instructions. 'Just say up! with feeling.' We practise flying around. Wonderful fun.

Lunch is at 12pm with the rest of Gryffindor. We have loads of different kinds of food, the table is full of chips, chicken and burgers. Later on, I hang out with Harry and Ron in the common room. (After I've done my homework!) This is the time when Harry, Ron and I talk to each other and discuss our secrets because we know we can trust each other.

Tea is really special as it is Hallowe'en. There are loads of sweets and candy.

After all that food, I'm sleepy. Off to bed, but is it . . . isn't that another knock at the door? Not another night creeping around the corridors of Hogwarts.

Kimi Patel (11)
Victoria Junior School, Wellingborough, Northants

HARRY POTTER

I was woken up by Ron shouting in my ear.
'Wake up!'
'Okay.'

I dashed to the bathroom, washed and dressed into my black robe. I rushed down to a breakfast of bacon, chips and sausages.

The post came. I had a parcel. I opened it, it was a broomstick, a Nimbus 2000! I was amazed. I never got mail. It was painted dark brown, but who sent it?

I got ready for my dark arts lesson. I was late. Professor McGonagall told me off. Next lesson was spells. I burnt my feather. I needed a new one!

Lunch. I ate earwig toads and Hermione ate her chocolate toads. My next lesson was flying. Madam Hooch told me to stay on the ground, but I didn't listen to her and I bashed myself into the wall!

Afterwards Ron and I played wizard's chess. I was terrified when the queen smashed the knight to pieces! I was at my potions lesson with Snape. I never knew any answers to the questions he asked me!

I decided to look for Hagrid. He told me about a chant swish and flick.

At dinner I ate chicken and salad. I went to sleep thinking about the chant!

Sonia Patel (11)
Victoria Junior School, Wellingborough, Northants

A DAY IN THE LIFE OF THE SCHOOL FIELD

One windy day in November, I (the school field) was singing to myself, forgetting it was Tuesday which was the worst day of the week. In came the children, skipping through the bright green gate. Oh no, the little ones are coming onto me! Then the whistle blew. Help, that scared me! Everybody ran to line up, chattering and talking. They gave me a headache. Off they went into their classes.

How much worse can it be? Then suddenly, out of nowhere came the grass cutter. Imagine having all your hair cut off. I wonder what the date is today. Uh oh, it's fireworks night. They're going to have a special night on me with fireworks going off. Oh no, all the daisies are disappearing. Ow! That was my hand. At last he stopped cutting.

What's the time? It's lunchtime. Out they came, the little monsters, never thinking about what it must be like being trampled on like you were lying down having a herd of elephants on your head. Oh no, they have skipping ropes. Ouch! It was like being walloped, but worse.

Rest at last, while they are doing their work after lunch. It's quarter past three and they're coming to watch the fireworks. Bang! *Bang!* Bang! I don't like this. Good, it's the last one! Off they go home at last.

Hannah Cooke (7)
Watton-At-Stone Primary School, Hertford, Hertfordshire

A Day In The Life Of My Shoe

I was sitting on the shoe rack asleep, then I heard a noise. It was Big Foot. He opened the door, slipped me on, got his bag out and went to school. When we went inside, he put his bag on the peg and went into the classroom. He sat down on his chair and flicked me off.

Mrs Berry started teaching and I was off, flung under the table two yards away and I fell down. I was hurt. He slipped me on and stuck his feet in and squashed me. It was play time. Finally he swapped into his trainers and ran to the field. I was left in the classroom where I fell asleep. I could hear them shouting and playing football. They came in. He swapped his shoes and went in and George Bateman stood on me. It hurt. I hoped he would not do it again, but he did. Hey, that hurt, help! Then they went to PE and put me in the bag.

Joe Dix (8)
Watton-At-Stone Primary School, Hertford, Hertfordshire

A DAY IN THE LIFE OF A PENCIL

It's early in the morning. I'm in the pencil pot with no lead at all. I hope I don't have to go in the horrible pencil sharpener. Okay, here they come. Oh no! Maria is taking me to be sharpened. Okay, here I go. Ahhh! She shouldn't have stopped to talk to Charlotte. Ah, here comes Mrs Berry. 'I'm here, I'm in here, come and pick me up.' Then she notices me and picks me up.

Oh no, she is putting me under the tap to wash off all the glue and mess I am covered in. I come out and I am soaked with water. Mrs Berry dried me off with a paper towel. Phew, it's play time at last. I am back on the table. Now I have a little while to get myself together since I've been in the bin.

Oh no! Here they come again. Darren has picked me up. Oh no! That hurt. Darren has slammed me on the table. Phew. The day is over and I can just relax. Ahhh, Mrs Berry has picked me up. It's the day when she changes the pencils. *Wheee*. I'm flying to another pencil pot, now I can relax.

Jessica Lo Monaco (8)
Watton-At-Stone Primary School, Hertford, Hertfordshire

A DAY IN THE LIFE OF A SCHOOL COMPUTER

I was sitting quietly on my mat, minding my own business, and then the afternoon came. All the children rushed to go on the computer. Oh no, here comes a hand, it's clicking and tossing me about everywhere. Oh look, they are going on Microsoft Word, that's my worst programme on the computer because you use the mouse lots and lots of times and it gives me a headache.

Finally, they've gone. Oh no, I forgot class 3 have to have their turn first. I can't believe it, they have gone on Microsoft Word like everybody else.

I hate being a computer mouse, it's so boring and silly because all you do is sit around sleeping all day long until people or children come and wake you up and really annoy you. When they go, it's lovely and peaceful. But nearly every afternoon, people come and wake me up, that's what's so annoying and boring.

Yippee, it's nearly home time for all the children. At last we get to be turned off and we can have a sleep.

Louis McPherson (7)
Watton-At-Stone Primary School, Hertford, Hertfordshire

A Day In The Life Of My School Shoes

I'm safe in the wardrobe in bed with her clothes, when suddenly she burst open the door and put her very small feet into me. I hope she's got clean socks on. Oh no! She is pulling my beautiful straps with Velcro and she's so hard at pulling, it's making me hurt. Oh no! It's the dreaded walk to school.

One hour later she's noticed that her insole is slipping. She's taking it out. Oh no, this tickles. Hey, stop it! This time her friend has taken me and she is running so fast that she dropped me. All my polish has come off. Jessica is really worried. I wonder what her mum has got to do to me. I hope she's not going to throw me away in the very stinky dustbin!

15 minutes later, phew, end of play time. It's almost time to go home, just 10 more minutes to go. Now, time to go home, aah! Jessica's taken me off and put me in my bed in the wardrobe for me to sleep until tomorrow.

Jessica Barrows (7)
Watton-At-Stone Primary School, Hertford, Hertfordshire

A DAY IN THE LIFE OF SOX

At the break of dawn I woke up and flexed my claws. A minute later I went to my owner's door and miaowed. Suddenly the children's door burst open. The older one shot to the bathroom. Two hours later the younger one came out of bed and brushed her teeth. I ran downstairs to eat my breakfast. Oh no! It's boring old tuna. I much prefer rabbit. I would even catch one.

At 3.20, the youngest owner came in. Suddenly she scooped me up. Oh no, she was swaying me from side to side. Ouch, hey be careful with me. Ding dong. Oh, there's someone at the door. It was Jessica Barrow at the door.

Five hours later the children had gone to bed. I wondered what the mother and father were doing. They were watching TV. I thought, I know, I'll go and sit on their laps. Ah, nice and soft. Hey! Don't shove me off, I've got feelings you know. Oh well, that's another day ended.

Alexandra Smith (8)
Watton-At-Stone Primary School, Hertford, Hertfordshire

MY TEDDY

I wake up in the morning and I have been kicked out of the bed by Hannah. She takes me down the stairs, dragging me by the arm. I feel every bump down the stairs. Then she takes me to the kitchen for Hannah's breakfast. Hannah has Coco Pops, but Hannah does not eat it, she spills it on me. I know that Hannah is not going to clean me up. I will smell later. I am cross with Hannah.

Hannah's brother wants to play WWF with me, but Hannah saves me because she knows I don't like it. She kicks Tom hard and takes me to bed and makes me go to sleep. She reads me a story. Then she goes to school, but I am bored. I walk around the house and I go to get a cup of tea and a biscuit. I have to run upstairs because Hannah is home from school. Ohhh, Hannah has to do her homework, so I think I will go to bed.

Hannah Cunningham (8)
Watton-At-Stone Primary School, Hertford, Hertfordshire

A DAY IN THE LIFE OF A SCHOOL RULER

One Friday morning it was a very sunny day. There was a pencil pot by the window in class 3. There was a ruler and that ruler is what I'm writing a short story about. Today however, to the ruler, when all the chairs are up, it's like he's in a jail. When all the chairs crash down, he knows that the children are coming into the classroom. 'Oh no, all the children are coming in. Soon I've got to hide.' Quickly he got into the bottom of the pencil pot. 'Hopefully they won't find me here.'

Suddenly there was a loud noise. 'Ahhhhh! This can't happen. The children are coming.' In the children come. They're making very loud noises. 'I think the chances are 90% I'm going to get picked up and 10% I'm not.' The children came in. Someone was right beside him, and guess what happened, he got picked up! 'Get off me, just get off me and stop being cruel, bending me backwards and forwards. Ahhhh! I'm snapped in half. Stupid boy. Don't put me in the bin. Oh well, I will have to live in the bin.'

Michael Searle (7)
Watton-At-Stone Primary School, Hertford, Hertfordshire

A Day In The Life Of A Pencil

Ahhh, it's Wednesday, the crack of dawn. No one's here but they will show up. Look, they're in the playground right now. Well class 3 aren't, they're in the cloakroom. Two seconds later, Michael picked me up and went to sharpen me. 'Ouch! My head,' I exclaimed! Then, for some reason, Michael put me back into the pencil pot, but then Charlotte threw me in the bin.

I heard someone calling, it was Jessica. She wanted a pencil. Super hero to the rescue. I tried to fly out of the bin and back into the pencil pot, but as I did so I banged into the tap and fell down the drain. Finally they went out to play, that gave me time to get out of the drain. Oh no, here they come to sharpen me again for tomorrow. *Ding.* Mrs Berry said it was home time, so they all went home. Ahhh, 3.15, time to rest.

Oh no, it's Thursday! This time Hannah's picked me up and she's throwing me against the wall. 'Please don't do it anymore. You'll put me on crutches.' She just ignored me! What a day.

Maria Wilkie (7)
Watton-At-Stone Primary School, Hertford, Hertfordshire

A Day In The Life Of A School Pencil

At the start of the day, I'm in the pencil pot and here come the children. Oh no, here comes Louis, he always breaks my lead and then I have to go in the horrible pencil sharpener. Luckily he dropped me. Here comes Ashley, he's even worse, he flings me across the room.

Ding-dong! Phew, it's play time at last. I'll have a rest now. Oh no, they're coming in already. I hope Mitchell picks me up because he's funny. Jake's got me, he's just as good. No, no, don't give me to Charlotte, she's going to give me a wash. Too late. After a wash I have to go in the pencil sharpener again. Once I was slammed in the pencil pot after being kicked across the floor. It's finally time to go home and I have a long sleep.

Dominic Bateman (8)
Watton-At-Stone Primary School, Hertford, Hertfordshire

A DAY IN THE LIFE OF HARRY POTTER

One day Harry was walking down to his friend's house. When he got there, Hermione said, 'Let's go and get Ron and we can have a stroll in the forest.' So they went into the forest, but because it was winter it got cold and dark and they got lost. Soon they came to a very misty clearing. When they came closer they found it was a graveyard.

Harry said, 'I am going to say a prayer,' and that's what he did. A few seconds later, something amazing happened.
Saint Nicholas came out of the grave that Harry was kneeling on, then he said in an oily voice, 'The forest is not safe for you, leave at once!' After that he went back into his grave. Suddenly there was a slithering noise.

'It came from that tree,' said Hermione. They came closer. Just at that very moment a black figure came up and jumped at them. It had no legs or anything. It was trying to kill them. They ran all the way home. When they got back their mums were there and they lived happily ever after.

Nicola Bramley (8)
Watton-At-Stone Primary School, Hertford, Hertfordshire

A DAY IN THE LIFE OF A DETECTIVE

I am a well known detective called Max Ford. I live in a small house next to the George and the Dragon pub. As I was taking a sip of beer, a man in crutches came in and asked to see me. 'How can I help you?' I asked.

'Three mountaineers have been killed. A mountain dog did it,' said the man. 'By the way, my name is Richard Everton,' he said.

'Come into my house, I need some evidence to believe you.'

In my house, he said, 'I went looking for mountaineers, but the mountain dog bit my leg off.'

He showed me a diary that the mountaineers had written. On the last page it had bloodstains. It read, 'Meet me at the wood at 11 o'clock at night. Meet me in the wood with the barber, Michael Jackson, Homer Simpson and Linsey Camelhead.'

They had weapons like machine-guns. In the forest at 11.05pm, every ten trees they passed, someone went missing. I turned around and I was the only one left. I turned back and ahhhhh!

Max Ford (8)
Watton-At-Stone Primary School, Hertford, Hertfordshire

GUILTY

She couldn't believe she'd just done that, why was she doing this? She quietly thought in her head as she came back from the bridge. She slowly walked home, trying to forget what she had done, but how could she? How could she push an innocent man off a bridge? Lucy was a lonely 20-year-old who had nothing and she'd just gone and made matters worse.

As Lucy got ready for bed, she heard noises in her bedroom. She quietly crept in but there was nothing there. She could have sworn she heard something. She walked away from her bedroom and then *smash!* Lucy ran into her room, but all there was was a broken vase on the floor, no person. Soon after, her wardrobe started to open and all her clothes were being thrown in the air and on the floor.

Lucy was startled by the ghost. She'd never believed in ghosts before but she knew something was wrong. The ghost wrecked everything. He messed up her bed and smashed all of her make-up. The dark voice said, 'You killed me, so for that I'll kill you, arrrgggg!'

Bethany Jackson (10)
West Haddon Endowed CE Primary School, Northampton

BIRTHDAYS

I ran downstairs. I was so excited. I turned the light on but there were no decorations, no fuss, no presents, no cards, nothing! Just a normal day.

My mum came down, but there was still nothing. 'Mum, you do know it's my birthday?'
There was a pause, Mum looked blank. 'Oh yes, I got you something. Here.' Mum handed me something.
'Socks!' I paused. I saw the expression on Mum's face. 'I mean socks, how lovely.'

I quickly escaped from the awkward silence up to my room. Socks, I thought to myself. She always does such exciting things for my birthday.
'Sophie!' my mum called from downstairs.
I plodded down miserably, hoping she wouldn't ask me to do the washing up or clean my room.
'I'm just popping out, can you come with me?'
I got my shoes on and walked to the car.

We arrived at a theme park.
'This is your birthday present.'
I was so pleased. I ran all the way in without paying. I had a great day. Well, that was the story of my birthday.

Sophie Blair (10)
West Haddon Endowed CE Primary School, Northampton

LOST AND FOUND

'Della, Della where are you?' Tom said. He was looking everywhere.
'You're supposed to find me Tich.'
Tom did not like the name 'Tich' but he answered to it anyway.
'You two come in now!' their mum said.
Della was twelve. She was Tom's older sister. Tom was only five.
'Ooh, what's for dinner?' Tom said.
'Chicken.' Their mum looked at Tom. 'Sorry, same again,' their mum said.

Della looked like skin and bones, literally. There was nothing of her. They lived in an old cottage in the middle of the forest. One day Della and Tom went out on a walk and they bumped into an old woman carrying a small basket. 'Hello child, what good news I bring, if you follow me you will be rich.'
So they followed her into a big house. They heard a bat fluttering around. 'Argghh! Get this bat out of my face.'
'How is my daughter Jenna?' the woman asked.
'What do you mean?' Della said.
'She is my daughter, your mum.'

Della lead her to the cottage. 'Hello love.'

Christy Connoll (9)
West Haddon Endowed CE Primary School, Northampton

SEAN TO THE RESCUE

One day there was a boy called Sean. Sean was really excited because tomorrow he was going on holiday. The next morning, Sean woke up really early. Sean was tired and bored on the journey, there was a traffic jam on the motorway.

Halfway, they stopped at the side of the road for a picnic. Later on they got there and went to the beach, but you couldn't swim in the sea because there were sharks. Far out in the distance, Sean saw something swimming around.

The next morning Sean went back to the beach and the swimming thing had gone and people were allowed in the sea. He went in but he did not go in by himself, his dad went in with him. Sean saw a patch of blood, then he saw a dead body where a shark had bitten a man.

Sean's dad spotted something splashing in the distance. Sean looked carefully and it was a little boy. Sean's dad went to get help while Sean waited and waited. He couldn't wait any longer and he swam out to sea. He dived under the water and grabbed the little boy. A lifeboat came with Sean's dad in it. Sean put the boy in the boat and got in before the sharks came.

Tom Humphreys (10)
West Haddon Endowed CE Primary School, Northampton

GEORGE TO THE RESCUE

Tom, who couldn't swim, and George who was very rich, were off to France. They couldn't wait. Tom was a bit nervous at first, but when they set off, he got over it. In the car they played loads of games and George's mum and dad didn't mind. The boys got onto the ferry and got something to eat. Then they went to the computer games and met a friend who was very spoilt. After a few games they went to the top bit of the boat and went outside.

A terrifying thing happened to Tom. He fell into the sea. George looked around and grabbed hold of a rope and dived straight in. The water was extremely cold, so he acted quickly. He was getting really scared, he searched everywhere for Tom, then he looked back and saw a red coat. George swam down to it, it was Tom. He pulled him up to the top. George put a towel around him and when they got to France he said, 'I'm not going on a ferry again,' and everyone laughed.

Nick Dixon (10)
West Haddon Endowed CE Primary School, Northampton

WALLED UP!

'Agnis, are you up there? Come down at once and eat your porridge!'
Agnis didn't want to get out of bed. She didn't want to get dressed or eat her breakfast.
'Agnis, now!'
Agnis quickly got dressed and grabbed her teddy bear, Petunia. 'I don't want to go.'
'Please don't be like this! We have to go to see if they are going to put an end to the black death!'
'But I'm scared.'
'Look, just eat your porridge.'
She ate up her food and tried very hard not to cry. As her mother was getting her purse, Agnis started to whimper.
'Look lovie,' started her mother, 'black death is a very serious illness and it needs to be wiped out before the whole city of Edinburgh die!'

It was very busy in the town square. People shouted from under the ground, pleading to let them out and that they were nearly better! Agnis felt sorry for them and leaned over, forgetting she had her teddy bear in her hands. She dropped it. 'Petunia!' She tumbled down the stairs and grabbed her toy. She ran back, but it was dark. She had been sealed up with the diseased people! 'Mother, Mother, Mother.'

Katherine Cory (10)
West Haddon Endowed CE Primary School, Northampton

WINGING IT

I had exactly planned on becoming an angel, but I hadn't planned on dying young, but then you don't do you? So I'm going to tell you about my life as an angel.

I arrived in Heaven and I walked towards some gates. There was a sign saying, 'Angel Academy'. I walked into the academy.

The children were wearing the same logo. A girl said to me that we needed to go for assembly to find out what class we were going to be in.

Then the headmaster said, 'Lola Price and Melanie Harp to Mr Cap.'
I thought, me, how do you know my name? Lola showed me the way to our beds. Finally we arrived. I thought to myself, hammocks. So I said to Lola, 'We're not sleeping here are we?'
'Yes,' she said.

Bedtime came and I heard a noise. Wings were coming out from behind my arms. All of a sudden, a lady appeared and said, 'I'm going to teach you to fly.'

I tried to fly but I couldn't. I just fell out of the sky. I knew I had a long way to go before becoming an angel.

Laura Moss (10)
West Haddon Endowed CE Primary School, Northampton

WOLF BOY

Once there was a boy called Robert. He was just a normal boy. His mum and dad were working and couldn't pick him up from school, so he had an au pair.

One night his parents were at a party and his au pair, called Simon, was asleep. He slipped out of his house to check out a haunted castle. Oh yes, Simon was wearing earplugs so he couldn't hear a thing.

As soon as he stepped out the door, he saw a laser beam come right at him and he started to turn into a werewolf. His skin started to grow thick brown fur.

He ran into the castle so no one would see him. Well, if they did they would just run away. As soon as he stepped in the door, he saw a spiral staircase. It was like a big curved snake. He quietly climbed the creaky stairs.

There, he saw a big laboratory and in it was a big spaceship where some green, slimy aliens emerged. They zapped him with a big laser gun and he woke up in his bed. He thought it was a dream, but he found a piece of wolf hair and realised it wasn't.

Lauren Towler (9)
West Haddon Endowed CE Primary School, Northampton

BACK IN TIME

One day in London, a boy named Josh went to the library. He went every Tuesday and he got a book for the week.

It was Tuesday today and he looked in the history section. He opened a book - The Ancient Egyptian. Before he knew what had happened, he was in Egypt.

He was surrounded by pyramids and guards with whips walked past with slaves. Josh was frightened and he had no idea what to do. The guards had caught him and they took him to the biggest pyramid to be locked away, but suddenly he was in the middle of World War II.

The siren went off, *rrrrrrrr!* Josh could hear lots of gunshots in the air. He raced to find shelter, but there was nowhere to go. Wait a minute, the underground, he thought. He found lots of people everywhere, he ran down the stairs and the place was crowded with people. He was frightened because everyone else had their mums there, but his wasn't.

Bang! He was in the Roman times and there were millions of warriors on both sides charging towards him. Next minute he was back in the library.

Daniel Lenton (9)
West Haddon Endowed CE Primary School, Northampton

A BEST FRIEND

Becky hurried towards the bus stop. The rain splashed her light brown hair and her pale face, but her face had been wet long before the rain touched it. She had been crying and she still was. She also had a stitch, her body was thumping like a big stick hitting her from inside.

She ran the last little way to the bus stop. Finally she got there. Her friends laughed at her, except one, Gary. Normally Gary always laughed at her, but why didn't he laugh this time? Becky was confused. She went and sat next to him, he was being very kind all of a sudden, and he gave her a tissue. He looked after her at school and she had a much better week after that. Gary never laughed at another person again.

Alexander Linnell (8)
West Haddon Endowed CE Primary School, Northampton

THE HAUNTED CASTLE

The castle stood on a great hill with a twisty flight of steps going up to it from the car park below. A hundred and ninety-nine steps the guide book had said, and the children intended to count them all.

When they all eventually got to the drawbridge, in one piece, since someone nearly fell down, they raced across the drawbridge, knocking the teacher in the moat.

'Children, first we're going to the dungeon,' said the teacher.
'Shall we lock her in it?' muttered two of the children.
'Come on children,' said the teacher who had already set off on the way towards the dungeon.
'Wicked thumbscrews, stretcher, Iron Maiden, execution, block, gallows and ball and chain,' said the children excitedly.
'Come on, we're going for a look in the lord's bedroom.'
There was a big, posh, four poster bed, a golden box with a map, a goblet and a few coins piled up. *Creak, thud.* 'What's that under the bed?' said the teacher.

They rushed along the battlements, nearly knocking two people off the side. They quickly rushed along the drawbridge and away from the castle.

Josh Bradley (8)
West Haddon Endowed CE Primary School, Northampton

THE FUNERAL

Becky hurried towards the bus stop. The rain splashed her light brown hair and pale face, but her face had been wet long before the rain had touched it. She had been crying and still was.

Her mother walked slowly with her father following. Becky stepped onto the muddy stairs of the bus. She waited for her parents to catch up and then entered the busy interior of the bus. She closed her brown eyes tightly, swallowed hard and bravely stepped further into the bus. Becky tiptoed up the red winding stairs to the second deck of the bus. It was quieter up there. Becky timidly sat down. Becky's mum and dad trekked up the stairs, looking like walking was hard. Finally the bus' engine rumbled and started. The travel was dramatic, then the brakes screamed to a halt.

Becky, her mum and dad climbed slowly out of the bus to the scene of an old crumbling church. The funeral. Becky's grandma had died.

The funeral was even more dramatic. Becky was asked to say a small speech, but cried so much that she could no longer speak.

When Becky left the church, her eyes again filled up with tears and she started crying.

When she got home, her friends talked to her and even though she was sad, she'd got happy memories.

Amy Vincent (9)
West Haddon Endowed CE Primary School, Northampton

THE MAGICAL BOOK OF SPELLS

Once upon a time, there was a girl named Louise. One night her mother Mary had put her to bed, but Louise could not sleep. She looked under her bed where she kept all her toys, but she couldn't find any. As she looked at the back of her bed, she saw this shiny thing. She reached her hand to the back of the bed and pulled out this shiny thing. It was a book. She opened it and to her surprise, glittery stuff came out and it swept her inside the book.

She found herself in a forest and there, standing next to her, was a witch. Louise screamed as she was quite frightened that the witch might turn her into a frog. She didn't though.

The witch said, 'Don't be frightened dear, my name is Witch Maya. You can call me Mary if you like sweetie.'
'Please don't call me sweetie and dear, my name is Louise.'
'Okay, now come and see my house, it's a cottage,' said the witch.

'In the wood it's lovely,' said Mary. 'Would you like to come and live with me for the rest of your life?'
'What would my mum say?'
'I have a magic book, so you can see your mother every day.'
So Louise said, 'Yes.'

They lived happily ever after.

Catherine Haley (8)
West Haddon Endowed CE Primary School, Northampton

ON A STRANDED ISLAND

Richard Taylor closed his eyes, but it didn't help. The bus had just hit a patch of ice and was sliding to the right.

It veered across the frozen surface towards the safety rail. The rail broke. Half a mile away you could hear screams. They all swam, but Millhouse couldn't swim. Jorg swam back to him.

Millhouse shouted, 'Help.'
Jorg got him as he was his friend. Jorg found an island. He thought, this will be great, we will be a tribe. We will build a tree house, we will live like kings. We will have a feast every night - chicken turkeys and warthogs.

Alec Elliott (8)
West Haddon Endowed CE Primary School, Northampton

999

Richard Taylor closed his eyes, but it didn't help. The van had just hit a patch of ice and was sliding to the right. It veered across the surface towards the safety rail. It hit the rail, overturned and shuddered to a halt.

Lucy-Ann sat whimpering in a corner, while Dad, in the driving seat, sat muttering. 'Richard,' he said, 'do you think that you could breathe in and fit through that small gap in the side of the van?'

Richard closed his eyes and hoped this was a nightmare.
'Okay, I'm out,' Richard shouted.
'Okay,' said Dad. 'Now look at both sides of the road and check for signs. Do you see any?'
'No,' Richard replied. 'But I remember seeing one for a phone box a few miles back.'
'Okay,' Dad said, 'go back then. Dial 999 and ask for the police. Now *go!*'

Richard stumbled along the narrow forest road and tripped over a tree root. This hurt. Blood was dripping down his leg and there were stones in it. Richard staggered along. He came to a phone box. '9 . . . 9 . . . 9,' he muttered. 'We will be with you soon.' Richard sank down in a corner. 'Phew,' he said.

Charlotte Porter (9)
West Haddon Endowed CE Primary School, Northampton

THE SILENT RIDER

The horse and rider galloped into the darkness. As the cyclist rode, the horse knocked him into a ditch. A fence impaled the cyclist and killed him.

Mark was climbing a tree and saw the cloaked rider, but two minutes later, the rider and horse disappeared. Scary, Mark thought.

The next day, Mark told all of his friends, but they didn't believe him. 'Meet me in the old watchtower tonight,' Mark said, opening a toffee and about to chew.

That night, at nine, they all met. Two hours later, Jack got up and said, 'This is stupid!' He got up and went to the path. He could hear the horse galloping towards him. The rider hit him at great speed and then the rider disappeared into the darkness.

Tom Drabble (10)
West Haddon Endowed CE Primary School, Northampton

SAINT NICHOLAS

John rushed down the stairs, splitting at the seams with excitement. Bursting through the door, he looked around the living room, the smile vanishing from his face. Where were the presents? Of course, the Christmas decorations weren't up. He and his mum were putting them up later. Disheartened, he turned round and yelled up the stairs, 'Mu-um, where are the presents?'
Slowly, a groggy looking lady in a dressing gown came out of a bedroom. John's mum. 'I don't know, Santa must have judged you to be a bad boy,' replied his mother slowly.

Sadly, he jumped down on the sofa and reached for the television remote, but before he touched it, there was a loud *bang* and a short, fat man appeared in front of the fire. Entirely clad in red, he could only be one person - Saint Nicholas.

'Howdy,' said Santa, bowing. 'I've come to give you your Christmas present.' John's mother was as surprised at this as John was. 'Take my hand and you will get your reward for being a good boy all year long.'

Shocked, John touched Father Christmas' hand, and with a small 'pop' went off on the biggest treat in all his life . . .

Philip Withnall (11)
West Haddon Endowed CE Primary School, Northampton

MILLY THE OTTER

Just call me Milly. I'm an otter. I live with my parents in a hole in the ground. We had just moved house. I was extremely scared because I had just found out that there were mink nearby. As you know, mink eat otters. My mum and I were going to swim over to see Nanny and Grandad. I had been scared at first.

When we got to the other end of the pond, I heard a weird nose. It sounded like it was trying to catch something in the pond. When I went to see what it was, it started snarling and then I saw it was a mink. 'Ah, there's a mink.' My mum came over and suddenly she grabbed me.

When we got to Nanny and Grandad's house, my mum warned them about the mink. After we had been to Nanny and Grandad's we went to my cousin's house. It was very comfy in their house. We had a cup of cocoa and some biscuits, then we went back home. When we got there it was time for bed. When I was in my bed I heard a scuttling noise, it was the mink. I did not sleep well that night.

Emily Litchfield (11)
West Haddon Endowed CE Primary School, Northampton

THE VOICE WITH NO BODY

I couldn't believe what I had just seen. The question was spinning round and round in my head, who or what had caused the train to crash?

It was a beautiful day, but I still had to go to work. I picked up my bag and went to catch my train. The station was down the road from my house. I got on the train, it started to move. I was going to London for a job interview, but I never made it.

Suddenly there was a loud bang as the train came off the rails. It skidded to a halt then rolled down the hill.
Then a strange voice was heard. 'I've killed him and I'm going to kill you!' The voice chanted these words over and over again. All that I could hear was the voice getting louder and louder, until as suddenly as it came, it went and there was silence!

When I woke up I was in hospital being treated for burns along with all the other passengers. 'What happened?'
'You were in a train crash,' said one of the nurses. All I could think about was the voice. What had it meant?

Laura Biart (11)
West Haddon Endowed CE Primary School, Northampton

CHRISTMAS

I couldn't sleep, I was so excited. Every time I shut my eyes, it was like they automatically opened again. Suddenly, I heard noises downstairs. I jumped out of bed and ran down the stairs. I peeked through the door to the lounge. I saw a man dressed in a red and white suit. He had a big white beard. It was Santa!

I opened the door and ran in. I couldn't believe my eyes.
'Well, hello little one, what's your name?'
'My name's Max.'
'Nice to meet you Max, now how would you like to come for a ride on my sleigh with me and my reindeer?' asked Santa.
'Yes please, I would love to.'
So out we went into the garden. The sleigh was brilliant. It was gold. We got in and off we went.

It was brilliant up in the sky, I could see my whole town. It was great. After about an hour, we went back and landed in my garden. We fed his reindeer and even built a snowman! But then it was time for bed. I waved goodbye to Santa and off he flew.

Jake Toseland (11)
West Haddon Endowed CE Primary School, Northampton

THE CAPTAIN AND THE BOSUN

Once upon a time there were two boys who lived beside the sea. They loved watching the boats each day to see which ones were new.

One day they noticed a different yacht, it had blue sails and was made from fibreglass. Walking upon the deck they could see two people.

As they got nearer, the boys knew that the strangers were planning something. They had got a map of the local sea and were arguing about it.

One of the men had a very sore hand. It was bleeding. It stained the man bright red. 'Give them back!' snatched Peter, who was trying to look through his brand new binoculars at the harbour.

Mark had got the best position for look-out, lying on the clifftop. He was studying a new boat and noticed the men on board were fighting. 'Look!' hissed Mark, 'Something's happening on that yacht. Those two men are having an argument.'

The men were heading for the Captain's quarters, the bosun was wrapping his hand up in a cloth to stop the bleeding. He had cut his hand whilst he was diving. The captain was looking worried. The bosun was telling the captain that they should go to Chicago because he had found out that there was lost treasure.

Mark and Peter were happy at the news.

Katy Clarke
West Haddon Endowed CE Primary School, Northampton

THE CRIME OF SATAN

He couldn't believe it. He didn't know why he had done it, but it had cost him his freedom. He had killed a policeman. He was jailed without a sentence . . . for life. It was worse than hara-kiri.

Jin Tsanami-Harikawashi was a possessed 32-year-old. He did things he didn't want to do. He had got himself jailed for life by running over a policeman and other inhabitants. He didn't know what had made him do it, but it made him commit manslaughter.

Then he felt it again. His pain writhed with anger. Something gave him strength. He smashed a hole in the wall of the Japanese State Prison. Satan had possessed him again.

The next week, he was on his death chair. Then it came again. He snapped the straps, stuck his head into the doctor and pulled out his guts.

He was at an institute. Satan was almost in complete control. Then he was possessed again, but this time, he had grown wings and he smashed through the roof. Then an ancient healer appeared below. The satanised Jin fell while writhing in pain to the ground. Jin was free, but he still died.

Andrew Wright (11)
West Haddon Endowed CE Primary School, Northampton

FIRST TRUE FRIEND

It was my first day there. I was so nervous, my heart was beating like a ball bouncing up and down. 'Annabel, come on, it's time to go!' said Mum.

We arrived there, the gates were wide open. I entered the room, all eyes were set on me. I sat down and got on with the maths set out in front of me.

Break soon came. I was sat on my own. I saw some people pointing and laughing at me. I felt like I wanted to cry.

'What's wrong?' said a gentle, kind voice. I explained to her what was wrong. She said, 'Don't worry, I'll stick by you.'
From this day on we have been friends. She stuck by me no matter what and was always there for me and made me feel welcome. She said that she had been through the same thing, but she had no one there for her, so she moved school. At least now I had a friend that was there for me that I could trust, no matter what.

Lauren Ingram (11)
West Haddon Endowed CE Primary School, Northampton

DISAPPOINTED

I ran downstairs. I felt marvellous. I was so excited. I opened my eyes and turned on the light. There was nothing there, no Christmas tree or decorations, but I expected them to be there, with presents lying on the floor under the tree with name tags saying Helen. But there wasn't.

Then Mum came down and I looked puzzled. She asked what was wrong and I said I thought it was Christmas. 'Yes it is,' replied Mum. 'But where are the presents?' I asked.
There was a pause. I just ran upstairs because Mum looked shocked and she opened the dining room door . . .

It was amazing, the whole room was full of presents and decorations. It was lovely, I couldn't believe my eyes. 'Thanks Mum! You're the best.'

I was ever so sorry, but Mum forgave me and it was the best Christmas that I had had in years and then Mum told me she was having twins. I was happy for Mum and Dad.

Charlotte Walters (11)
West Haddon Endowed CE Primary School, Northampton

WHEELED FOR LIFE

I was gripping onto a cliff, clutching onto a branch. It had prickles, but if I let go I would fall to my death.

I was trying to swing up, but it was no use. I was almost dead because it was close to snapping. *Snap.* I fell. I was falling faster every second. I hit the ground. Luckily I was alive, but in a lot of pain, and I mean a *lot* of pain. I was starving and gasping for water. No one had noticed me, maybe because I was lying in a thorn bush, a very big thorn bush.

'Jake, Jake, are you alright?' When I opened my eyes I saw a face, not just any face, it was my mum.
'You're a very naughty boy,' bellowed my mum. 'You're only 11 and you're nearly dead. You have a lot more time left in your life. You're grounded.'

A doctor came towards me. 'You're going to be alright. However, you're going to be in a wheelchair all of your life.' Now I know never to climb and play on cliffs. I have learnt a lesson today.

Jake Hillery (11)
West Haddon Endowed CE Primary School, Northampton

THE TERROR OF THE NORSEMEN

More than 2000 years ago, the Norsemen from near Norway, Sweden and Denmark were great adventurers. They were known as Viking Raids.

Battling over beaches on foot, every step echoed on the crumpled pebbles. His name is Zak Vike the Brave. Gripping his shiny, sharp sword, he struggled up the steep hill, up towards the shining light in the distance. The treasure's mine, he thought to himself. As he burst through the door on the hut, he stopped in astonishment. His eyes looked at the lady in the corner of the hut, gripping onto her child, terrified what the future might hold.

As Zak entered the room, he noticed how bare it was. There was a simple wooden table and chairs. On the table there was a part-eaten loaf of bread and a bowl of soup. The family were obviously very poor. There was no treasure here. In his mind her face turned into the face of his wife and child back in Sweden. For once in his life that brave warrior turned away. It wasn't his day to kill. There was nothing here to kill for.

Lucy Rogers (10)
West Haddon Endowed CE Primary School, Northampton

WAS IT THERE?

It was there in the lounge. Was it somebody? Mum or Dad? Or was it something else?

There was a rustle, maybe it was a ghost, or a monster. I wasn't sure. I crept into the lounge. I listened, there was no noise, but then I saw it. The long, hairy thing scuttled along the floor. I ran upstairs, into my room and pulled the covers over my head in bed. I wanted it to be a dream.

It was the following morning, I jumped out of bed and plodded down the stairs, not remembering about the night before. I stood in the kitchen eating my breakfast, when suddenly from the lounge something moved. The thing reappeared. I dropped my bowl and screamed. Mum and Dad came crashing down the stairs.
'What's up?' asked Mum.
'It's over there!' I said.
'What's over there?' questioned Mum.
'The creature, it's a lion and a snake put together,' I answered.
Mum went.

It was 1 o'clock. I entered the lounge, it crept up on me.
'I'm going to do what you did to me!' growled the creature. His claws went into my neck.
I fell on the floor, bleeding to death. What I did to the thing, I'll never know.

Sarah Rotheram (11)
West Haddon Endowed CE Primary School, Northampton

THE HEADLESS HORSEMAN

I lay there awake, thunder was crashing. I could smell smoke. A baby was crying. I got up and looked out of the window. There was another crash of lightning. I screamed. There was a face at the window, no, I stand corrected, it was a neck. I looked again. It was gone but I could hear ghostly horses' hooves.

The next morning, I was still a bit shaken up. Vicky was standing there in her designer sunglasses smirking. 'I heard you screaming last night. Do you still believe in that headless horseman thing?' I ignored her, I didn't want to waste my breath. I walked straight past her into the stable to look after Polo.

When I walked in the horse at the very end of the stables began to go mad. Then Vicky came out and dared me to ride on the road where I first saw the headless horseman.

The night came. I had reached the road and mist was beginning to creep up. Polo started to panic and he bucked me off and galloped away. I began to hear horses' hooves and laughter. Evil laughter. I knew what it was.

Hannah Shaw (11)
West Haddon Endowed CE Primary School, Northampton

WORLD WAR II

When World War II started, I was only five years old. My mum was twenty-six. I don't know how old my dad was. One cold, foggy night, I was scared because all I could hear was howling and people screaming.

It was the middle of the night on a Saturday. That's the night when the most bombs were dropped over our city. I remember on that night we had to go down to the bomb shelter and I was really, really tired, more than I was the night before. I tripped up and Mum and Dad were already in the bomb shelter. They didn't know that I had tripped over a rock.

Suddenly there was a noise of a bomb near a local shop. I could hear from inside the bomb shelter: 'Where's Annie? Where's Annie?'
'Oh no,' said Mum.
'Mum, come here,' I said.
'Okay,' she said. All of a sudden another bomb dropped behind our house. Me and Mum had to quickly run into the shelter.
'Annie, where have you been?' said Dad.
'I tripped over a stone on the way in.' Another bomb dropped. Mum thought it was on our house . . .

Sam Owen (11)
West Haddon Endowed CE Primary School, Northampton

A MAGICAL NIGHT

Milly glanced around. The stately home she was visiting glowered above her. As she looked, one particular statue caught her eye. It was a large Griffin intricately covered with huge, ornate wings. 'Ohhh,' she breathed, touching his cold, stone body. Out came her beloved camera, then *click*, another memory saved forever.

Milly fell on the grass. 'Oh this heat,' she sighed. She stared lazily up into the summer sky . . .

Milly awoke with a start. The sun had set, and stars, not clouds, now filled the sky. She lent against the stone Griffin. 'I wish you were alive,' she said longingly.
'But I am!' said the Griffin, turning his head. Milly backed away, tripping over tree roots and stones.
The Griffin flew overhead and circled like a vulture before landing gently on her shoulder. 'Come,' he whispered, 'come with me.'

Slowly, hesitating slightly, Milly and her companion began to walk to the main lawn. As they arrived an amazing sight met their eyes. There in the centre of the lawn stood every creature Milly could have dreamt of. Gatherings of gods and flocks of fauns surrounded her as she mingled among them. The Griffin seemed to know every one of them and he frequently stopped to engage them in conversation.

They walked briskly along the tree-iined path leading from the lawn, passing on their way many amazing sights, and soon ventured into an ornamental garden.

While the Griffin was busy talking to a Cenataur, Milly watched with great interest the antics of the other creatures.

She looked on in amusement at several Greek women clustered around a tall, handsome man who kept flexing his muscles and preening himself. On the base he was standing on, Milly could just make out the name Hercules. Suddenly, a beautiful mermaid jumped out of a nearby lake and waved.

The Griffin spoke softly in her ear. 'Come quickly, there is no time to ponder.' He showed Milly to a small gap in the hedge. What Milly saw when she looked through made her gasp. There, in the glade, was a pure white unicorn. In the moonlight she saw it raise its head, then bolt into the bushes.

Suddenly the Griffin froze. 'Hurry, they are opening the gates!' he cried frantically. As they ran past, all the creatures seemed to be in the same state of panic as the Griffin.

As the gates of the house slowly opened, streams of people flooded in. Milly turned to speak to the Griffin, but he was once again a stone statue.

A few weeks later, Milly was looking through some photos when she came across the photo of the Griffin. As she looked closely at it, the Griffin turned its head and winked.

Milly smiled. She would never forget that night.

Sarah Brand (11)
Wilbury Junior School, Letchworth, Hertfordshire